A Touchdown in Reading

An Educator's Guide to Literacy Instruction

by

Kathryn Starke

ISBN: 9780976973782
Library of Congress Control Number: 2020910949

Printed in the United States

Published by Creative Minds Publications
www.creativemindspublications.com

Table of Contents

Dear Fellow Educators,

I have been teaching children to read for most of my life. When I was ten years old, I started my own tutoring business to support kindergarten children with their early literacy skills. Parents paid me to teach their young readers alphabet recognition, letter sounds, and rhyme patterns. As a teenager, I was a tutor, babysitter, nanny, and summer camp instructor. I graduated from Longwood University with a BS in elementary education eager to begin my teaching career. I could not wait to student teach; my first placement was in a suburban elementary school close to where I grew up.

I was excited to create hands-on activities to help young children learn. I vividly remember staying up late one night to trace, cut, and personalize piggy banks for the children to count out real coins and stamp coins in their "banks" the next day. The students loved the math lesson so much that I was already planning what to do next. My ideas were quickly squashed when my cooperating teacher told me that her students learned best by sitting quietly and completing worksheets; that is what she expected me to do. Feeling defeated, I took her manilla folder of approved match worksheets to use for the remainder of the weeks.

My second placement was in a sixth-grade social studies class in an inner-city middle school. My cooperating teacher was an incredibly inspiring educational leader; I was a nervous wreck when she told me I would be taking the lead. After my previous experience, I selected the best introductory geography worksheet for my initial lesson. The students did not agree. They talked over me, shouted at each other across the room, and threw balled up papers in the trashcan the entire time. I went home that Friday afternoon and cried. I woke up the following morning with a new perspective and an idea; I drove to the local teacher supply store to buy a globe patterned notepad. I went back home, turned on the radio, and wrote a personal note on every sheet of paper.

"And the whole world loves it when _____ _____."

                                                     student name   positive description or action

When the same group of disinterested, rowdy children walked into the classroom that Monday afternoon, I was blasting Outkast's current hit, *And the Whole World*. The students walked in dancing and singing. When the song ended, I explained to the class how each day I would be presenting an award to each student. *And the whole world loves it when Angel shares her ideas.* They cheered and asked each day when they would hear their name. It was evident that this particular group of students labeled "at risk" did not often hear positivity or feel appreciation.

Once the sixth graders realized how I saw them as unique individuals, they saw me in a different light too-a young teacher who wanted to help children achieve. They became excited to learn in the way that I wanted to teach (using songs, dance, stories, and games). I planned and implemented anything and everything I could to increase student motivation, engagement, and comprehension. At the end of the four and half weeks, the students presented me with a giant card in the shape of the earth with the following words. *And the whole world loves it when Miss Starke teaches our class.*

Of course, I cried again-this time with happy tears. I was offered a job at the middle school but had my heart set on teaching elementary school in the district. I sent out applications and received some interviews. During the process, I was told I was too nice to handle "their students" or that my teaching ideas were too out of the box. I found these comments so ironic since kindness and innovation are usually considered quality traits. I decided to apply to

Richmond Public Schools, an urban school district, in the city of Richmond, Virginia and was offered three positions on the spot. I took a second-grade position at an inner-city elementary school where students were bused in from around the city. One of my students actually rode the city bus our school every morning. I fell in love with this school community. The parents supported my vision of teaching, and their children loved coming to school.

Yes, in my school we experienced gun violence and death every year. On my very first day of teaching, a seven-year-old handed me a tiny square torn from the Richmond Times Dispatch, the local newspaper, that had three lines describing the seventy-third homicide of the year. She told me that was her father and asked for tape to display on her desk. Yes, many of our students lived in poverty. I kept Cheerios and juice boxes in my classroom for my starving children who did not get breakfast at home (and sometimes not even a real dinner).

We also had children read significantly below grade level in our school, something not unique to our school. According to the 2019 NAEP, only 37% of nine-year-old students read below grade level. That percentage decreases to 22% of nine-year-old students who live in low-income areas. When I recognized that my own second-grade students struggled in reading, I went back to school to get my master's degree in Literacy and Culture while teaching full-time.

I have focused my career on urban education, which is not always mentioned in the best light. More specifically, I help schools achieve reading success through implementation of urban literacy education. I have been a first, second, and third grade classroom teacher, reading specialist, district literacy coach, adjunct professor, and urban literacy consultant. I have helped failing elementary schools from Brooklyn, New York to Charleston, South Carolina achieve full accreditation, often in one year. Since I am unable to travel to every school every day, I am hoping this book will be the next best thing. I wrote this book for several reasons.

1-to provide proven strategies and lessons in reading instruction that can instantly be implemented into your classroom
2-to share personal stories from my own work in urban literacy education that hopefully remind you of the students or scenarios in your own school
3-to give you some personalized consulting along the way as you plan your literacy lessons.

Teaching reading is the most complex subject with often the least amount of support. As I prepare for publication of this title, our teachers have been tasked to provide quality reading instruction online and ensure all students have access to remote learning opportunities. Therefore, when schools finally resume, we will have so much work to do! This book provides lessons and activities that can be used for in-person and online learning experiences. Once a child can read, they can be successful in anything they do. Fifteen years later, I am still hearing from former students and their parents. Reading opens doors. Hopefully reading this book will provide you with inspiration and give you permission to create literacy lessons to help all children become life-long readers and writers.
Sincerely,
Kathryn Starke

Step One: Creating a Community of Readers

1. Motivation
2. Engagement
3. Building Background Knowledge
4. Differentiation
5. Communication

Whenever I walk into an elementary school or classroom, I instantly decide if I feel that this school community promotes a love of literacy. Most often, my conclusion is based on visuals including reading theme bulletin boards, series books graphs, or even a book vending machine. Other times, it is when I hear students begging to the go to the library or sneaking a chapter to read during a math lesson. I have observed that when five components are seamlessly implemented throughout a school year, a community of readers emerges. Students and parents recognize the importance and joy of reading when they see a teacher who loves literacy. When students entered my classroom on the first day of school, we read the following preamble. It was displayed on a poster and signed by every child in the class and me.

We the students in Miss Starke's class, in order to form a more perfect classroom: establish expectations, ensure a peaceful atmosphere, provide a positive learning environment, promote literacy, and secure a safe and respectful place for us all.

You can use the follow checklist to see if your own classroom or school currently promotes a love of literacy. What can you add to your own classroom this year?

Checklist: A Classroom that Promotes Literacy

o Books, books, books
o Reading Nook
o Bulletin Board
o Set Guided Reading/Small Group Instruction Table
o Poetry Notebooks
o Fluency Folders
o Word Wall
o Content Vocabulary Wall
o Phonics Wall/Sound Board
o Leveled Book Boxes
o Big Books
o Access to Grade Level Text
o Read Aloud Experiences
o Literacy Manipulatives (magnetic letters, sound boxes, pointers, etc.)
o Word Work Games (boggle, scrabble, rhyme cards, etc.)
o White Boards/Markers
o Anchor Charts
o Graphic Organizers
o Designated Writing Workshop Area
o Writing Portfolios
o Exit Tickets

Motivation is essential in everything that we do in life, especially when we are teaching children to read. We want children to be excited about reading. We want them to love books, which goes beyond the idea of book choice. Children do not learn to read simply by being given the freedom to choose whatever book they want to read. We need to allow children to set individualized, personal reading goals. A "forty book challenge" is extremely overwhelming to a reluctant reader. When we allow students to set attainable goals that they can achieve on their own, the motivation level increases. These goals may include a certain number of pages, minutes, chapters, or books. On the pages that follow, I have included a bookmark for students to document page numbers for you to use with your students during independent reading time.

Personal reading goals like these should not be tied to a parent signature or class goal. We are celebrating the reading growth of each child. When a goal is achieved, we must celebrate that accomplishment. Reading is no easy feat. Motivation helps us work faster and harder to reach a goal. Motivation is a part of life. As teachers, we are motivated by jean days or flex time at school. When we are hooking children on reading, they are motivated by reading rewards like a bookmark, an extra trip to the library, or reading to a kindergarten class. While children are reading to meet goals, they are increasing their reading. When children increase their volume of reading, their decoding, fluency, vocabulary, and comprehension skills also increase. Eventually, the intrinsic reward of loving reading is present, especially when students are no longer struggling in reading.

Another form of motivation is an event or a celebration of reading that evokes a pleasant emotion. When we recall a positive memory, we are happy; we want to continue doing what makes us happy. We want children to love the feeling of curling up with their favorite book. The literacy events on the following pages were created to give your school community a sense of happiness and comfort all year long. I want to see all of your events. Be sure to post photos and tag me on social media @KathrynStarke so I can celebrate with you.

My Pages of a Book Collection
(25-50-100-150-200-250-300-350-400-450-500)

Name: _____

Grade: _____ Teacher: _____

Date: _____ # of Pages Read _____

Date: _____ # of Pages Read _____

Total # of Pages Read to Date: _____

Date: _____ # of Pages Read _____

Total # of Pages Read to Date: _____

Date: _____ # of Pages Read _____

Total # of Pages Read to Date: _____

Date: _____ # of Pages Read _____

Total # of Pages Read to Date: _____

Date: _____ # of Pages Read _____

Total # of Pages Read to Date: _____

Date: _____ # of Pages Read _____

Total # of Pages Read to Date: _____

Date: _____ # of Pages Read _____

Total # of Pages Read to Date: _____

Date: _____ # of Pages Read _____

Total # of Pages Read to Date: _____

My Pages of a Book Collection
(550-600-650-700-850-900-950-1000)

Name: _____

Grade: _____ Teacher: _____

Date: _____ # of Pages Read _____

Total # of Pages Read to Date: _____

Date: _____ # of Pages Read _____

Total # of Pages Read to Date: _____

Date: _____ # of Pages Read _____

Total # of Pages Read to Date: _____

Date: _____ # of Pages Read _____

Total # of Pages Read to Date: _____

Date: _____ # of Pages Read _____

Total # of Pages Read to Date: _____

Date: _____ # of Pages Read _____

Total # of Pages Read to Date: _____

Date: _____ # of Pages Read _____

Total # of Pages Read to Date: _____

Date: _____ # of Pages Read _____

Total # of Pages Read to Date: _____

Motivational Book Page Log

I read _____ pages! I get _____!

25 pgs.=Reading sticker or stamp
50 pgs.=Literacy Certificate
100 pgs.=Bookmark
150 pgs.=Read in the teacher's chair
200 pgs.=Choose a special book from the classroom library to take home for the night
250 pgs.= Invite to a breakfast book club
300 pgs.=Get an extra trip to the library
350 pgs.=Enjoy independent reading time outside
400 pgs.=Invite to a literacy lunch
450 pgs. =Give the gift of reading by selecting a book from designated list/area to donate in your name to a classroom or school of your choice
500 pgs. =Read your favorite book to a K-2 class

Motivational Book Page Log

I read _____ pages! I get _____!

550 pgs.=Congratulatory letter from an author (Local authors are everywhere with social media.)
600 pgs.=Invite to a story character tea party
650 pgs.= Go on a fieldtrip to the public library
700 pgs.=Read a chapter or favorite book to your classmates for a readaloud experience
750 pgs.=Select a book to keep from the *Scholastic* order form
800 pgs.= Invite to an evening movie book night
850 pgs.=Get a shout out in school announcements, marquee, or social media
900 pgs.=Get a "sweet treat" at lunch
950 pgs.=Invite to an afterschool bookathon
1,000 pgs.=Awarded at end-of-school year academic assembly

Dear Reader,

Congratulations on reading 550 pages of some incredible books! What a wonderful accomplishment to celebrate. As an author and publisher, I love reading and writing. One of my favorite children's books of all time is *Where the Sidewalk Ends.* If you have not read this hilarious book of poetry by Shel Silverstein, I highly recommend it. Now get back to your book and keep reading!

Sincerely,

Kathryn Starke

Dear Reader,

Congratulations on reading 550 pages of some incredible books! What a wonderful accomplishment to celebrate. As an author and publisher, I love reading and writing. One of my favorite children's books of all time is *Where the Sidewalk Ends.* If you have not read this hilarious book of poetry by Shel Silverstein, I highly recommend it. Now get back to your book and keep reading!

Sincerely,

Kathryn Starke

Celebrating Literacy Throughout the School Year

Fall: Books for Breakfast/Book Fair (Grandparents or Parents)
    Bobbing for Books
    Pumpkin Portraits and Character Book Parade
    Book Tasting

Winter: Give the Gift of Reading
    Hot Chocolate and Chapter Books/Cocoa and Conversations
    Read Across America
    March Madness (Book Brackets)
    Tackle Reading Day

Spring: OSCARS (Our School Cares About Reading Success) Night
    One School, One Book
    One Million Minutes
    World Series of Reading
    Poetry Tea Party

Summer: Backpack of Books
    Special Delivery
    Beach Reads

Dear Teachers/Parents,

      We are celebrating a love of literacy this week. An extra special treat for students will be the opportunity to go "bobbing for books" during their reading block. Students will be able to select a special book to keep and add to their home library. Happy Reading!

Dear Teachers/Parents,

      We are celebrating a love of literacy this week. An extra special treat for students will be the opportunity to go "bobbing for books" during their reading block. Students will be able to select a special book to keep and add to their home library. Happy Reading!

Students, Teachers, and Parents
You are Invited to the

OSCARS

(**O**ur **S**tudents **C**are **A**bout **R**eading **S**uccess)

March _____
6:00-7:00 PM
School Cafeteria

*Come listen to the second graders read poetry
*Visit the writing workshop
*Put on a show with the reader's theater station
*Partner read from our selected titles
*Donate any new or gently used books to ROAR (Reach Out and Read, which provides books to clinics around the country to promote early literacy); the box will be in the lobby to drop off books

Come camera ready! See you on the red carpet!

Engagement is evident when students are excited about literacy and actually reading independently, with partners, or in small groups. When we develop engaging literacy lessons, students actively listen, participate, ask questions, and are eager to learn. When we match a student with a book that matches his or her interest level, engagement increases.

The book and movie industry understand that hooking fans through a series is a powerful way to increase sales and engagement. Once we find an author or series that we love, we keep going back for more. Implementing series book clubs, a genre study, or author studies are effective ways to get children hooked on reading. You will find some activities throughout the pages of this book that specifically support reading engagement including an author study.

Differentiation is essential when teaching reading. Children will not learn to read a text that is too difficult for them. Children will not increase their reading knowledge by always reading books that are too easy for them. We need to constantly track our student's reading journey. Therefore, we need to understand how to successfully match them with a "just right book" or instructional level text and independent level text.

Teachers are the best book matchmakers for their students. While teachers are building relationships with their students in the beginning of the year, they should conduct one-on-one interviews or give interest surveys to each child, depending on the grade level. This practice will help the classroom teacher learn the strengths, challenges, likes, and dislikes of every student.

This valuable information only helps teachers in selecting the best book to spark a child's interest in reading. In addition to teachers, no one knows more about someone's favorite things than their friends. With this in mind, classmates should also be encouraged to be book matchmakers and provide personalized book recommendations for their peers.

While student reading levels progress and interests change, book matchmakers continue to excite children about reading by strategically matching kids to an engaging text that they can both master and enjoy. When a child is paired with a book that matches both their interest and reading level, the magic of reading really begins.

Back to School Lesson: Host a book talk
1. Provide each student with an index card.
2. Student writes fiction or nonfiction in big letters on one side of the card.
3. On the back, the student writes their favorite genre or topic, favorite author or all-time favorite book (a comfort book like that always makes you happy like your comfort food), and the title of the last book they read.
4. The teacher instructs students with fiction cards to one side of the room and nonfiction cards to the other side of the room.
5. The students are to mingle with the others in the group like a "book cocktail party" sharing their index card information. The listeners should recommend a book title that matches their interests and preferences.
6. The goal is for each student to leave the circle with the next book they should read.

Book Talk!

- **Fiction or Nonfiction?**
- **Favorite Genre or Topic**
- **Favorite Author or All-time Favorite Book (Your Comfort Book)**
- **What is the title of the last book you read?**

Once students understand their role as a book matchmaker, the following book profiles can be copied and available in a book bucket or envelope in the classroom library to increase reading engagement.

Book Matchmaking Profile

Do you prefer fiction or nonfiction? _____

Favorite genre or topic _____

Favorite author or book _____

What is the last book that you read and loved? _____

_____

You have a book match!

Based on your profile, I believe you would like to read the following book:

Title _____

Author _____

My Reading Survey

Name_____ Date_____

1. What is your favorite picture book?

2. What is your favorite chapter book?

3. Do you prefer fiction or nonfiction books?

4. Who would you like to read a biography about?

5. What do you like to learn about from information books?

6. Who is your favorite author?

7. Is reading easy or hard for you?

8. What is one thing you want to learn more about in reading?

Hooking Kids on Reading

Fiction/Nonfiction Sort

Fiction	Nonfiction
fake, fun story, make believe	real, informational
beginning, middle, end	glossary
characters	heading
setting	caption
events	facts
dialogue	index

table of contents

Genre: exploring a variety of text

- Fantasy
- Mystery
- Biography
- Autobiography
- Informational
- Historical Fiction
- Realistic Fiction
- Science Fiction
- Poetry
- Traditional Literature (folktales, legends, fables, fairy tales, tall tales, and myths)

Genre Scavenger Hunt

Name _____

Directions: Search through your classroom or home library. Locate one title for each genre listed below.

1. Informational _____

2. Mystery _____

3. Realistic Fiction _____

4. Biography _____

5. Historical Fiction _____

6. Science Fiction _____

7. Poetry_____

8. Fantasy _____

9. Fairy Tale _____

10. Folk Tale/Traditional Literature _____

*Now, choose your favorite book from the library.

Is the book fiction or nonfiction? _____

What is the genre of the book? _____

How do you know? _____

Sample Author Study: Roald Dahl

The BFG
Boy: Tales of Childhood
Charlie and the Chocolate Factory
Charlie and the Great Glass Elevator
Danny the Champion of the World
Dirty Beats
The Enormous Crocodile
Esio Trot
Fantastic Mr. Fox
George's Marvelous Medicine
The Giraffe and the Pelly and Me
Going Solo
James and the Giant Peach
The Magic Finger
Matilda
The Minpins
Roald Dahl's Revolting Rhymes
The Twits
The Vicar of Nibbleswicke
The Witches
The Wonderful Story of Henry Sugar and Six More

Roald Dahl Book Quotations

Name _____ Date _____

Directions: Read the quotes below from popular Roald Dahl books. Match the quotation on the left to the book title on the right it comes from. Write the number of the quote on the line beside the correct title.

1. "The child will become a mouse."

_____ *George's Marvelous Medicine*

2. "What are you going to do now that you've read all the children's books?"

_____ *James and the Giant Peach*

3. "Just because I is a giant, you think I is a man-gobbling cannubully?"

_____ *The Magic Finger*

4. "It jumps out and touches the person who has made me cross."

_____ *The Witches*

5. "We will polish your glass til it's shining like brass and it sparkles like sun on the sea…"

_____ *Charlie and the Chocolate Factory*

6. "Oh Grandma, if you only knew what I have in store for you!"

_____ *The BFG*

7. "Right on the highest branch, it's growing Bigger and bigger. Go pick it!"

_____ *Matilda*

8. "Greetings to you, the lucky finder of this Golden Ticket from Mr. Willy Wonka!

_____ *The Giraffe and the Pelly and Me*

Book Unit: based on *Charlie and the Chocolate Factory*

by

Roald Dahl

A tasty unit for all grade levels!

Unit of Study Overview-
1. Read aloud one or two chapters a day to your class.
2. Decorate your door, hallway, bulletin board, or classroom.
(Examples include the following: visualization pictures, golden tickets displayed, a sign saying something like "Oompa-Loompas at Work")
3. Celebrate Dahlicious Dress Up Day
4. On-going Idea: Implement "golden tickets" as behavior rewards in the classroom

Ideas to Implement:
- Play WONKA (instead of BINGO) with sight words or vocabulary words
- Have a Candy Day (each child brings in a candy or candy bar) for the day's activities including tallying and graphing the candy and using all of the candy names to write a fictional story (ex: Kit Kat met her friend at Nestle Crunch Grille...)
- Write a recipe of a dessert with chocolate (real or new creation) to make a chocolate class cookbook
- Roald Dahl Author Study (make text to text connections, character charts, posters advertising each book, and group work discussions)
- Create/invent a new candy. Write up the description of the candy for the wrapper and create a wrapper for the candy. Advertise your candy and persuade your classmates why your candy is the best to purchase. Vote on the best candy campaign in the classroom.
- Research chocolate, candy making, chocolatiers, etc. Use websites, write letters, and ask experts to come and speak about their work.

Chapter by Chapter Ideas for Instruction

Introduction: Read the page introducing the five children from this book before reading. Assign a character to each child. Based on the description provided, the student must illustrate the character as they visualize. When the characters are introduced later in the book, return the illustration for them to add to their visualization.

Chapter 1: Children will write about their family (who they live with, where their parents work, and where they live). Compare themselves to Charlie.

Chapter 2: Write some questions that have popped in your mind about Willy Wonka's Chocolate Factory.

Chapter 3: Design, draw, and write a description about your own chocolate house.

Chapter 4: Based on the headline "Wonka Factory to be Opened at Least to Lucky Few", write an article about what you think that means and what is going to happen next.

Chapter 5: Create a golden ticket for a prize you would like to receive in your classroom.

Chapter 6: Use these character descriptions to add to original visualizations.

Chapter 7: Make a birthday list or write about a birthday tradition in your home.

Chapter 8: Use these character descriptions to add to original visualizations. Put all of the images together and created a Wanted Poster style bulletin board

Chapter 9: Play a probability game with dice. Predict how many times you will roll the number 1 then each child rolls five times to see who does.

Chapter 10: Write about what you like to do on a cold winter day.

Chapter 11: Decision making classroom conversation: Would you have kept the golden ticket or sold it? Why or why not?

Chapter 12: Write a letter to the person in your family you would choose to visit Willy Wonka's factory with you and explain the reason.

Chapter 13: Add to the character descriptions (if not completed) and display.

Chapter 14: Draw a picture of Willy Wonka and write descriptive traits around the image.

Chapter 15: Make a list of all of the desserts you can think of that contain chocolate.

Chapter 16: Draw your interpretation of an oompa-loompa.

Chapter 17: Create a new song (full of rhyme) for your class of oompa-loompa to sing (it can be about a unit of study in your classroom, this book, or something else).

Chapter 18: Use a map to locate the rivers in your hometown, state, or region, and determine the length of each river. Imagine the river of chocolate and see how long it would stretch across your area.

Chapter 19: Invent a new candy.

Chapter 20: Make a colorful gumball machine of at least ten gumballs (use construction paper and stencils to cut out circles). On each gumball, write rhyming words, synonyms, antonyms, homophones, etc. **can suggest gumball pairs in the same color to easily see the antonyms, homophones, rhyme pair, etc.

Chapter 21: Write the breakfast, lunch, or dinner menu you'd like to have of the chewing gum meal.

Chapter 22: Use smelly stickers to create a fantasy story.

Chapter 23: Brainstorm candies, desserts, and treats that fall under each geometric shape and sort them on a class chart. Ex: square=brownies, circle=M&M's, rectangle=Nestle crunch bar, sphere=scoop of ice cream, etc.

Chapter 24: Would a squirrel be a good pet? Can you train a squirrel to be a pet? Is a squirrel considered a tame animal? Research squirrels to find out.

Chapter 25: What name would you give another floor option on the elevator ride? What would you do in that location?

Chapter 26: What are some common food commercials on television currently? Think of them and describe the object so a classmate can guess. Example Clues: smells like syrup, round, design looks like a beehive. Answer: Eggo Waffles

Chapter 27: Think back to the original list of children; only Charlie remains. What was the cause and effect for each of the other children to now be gone?

Chapter 28: Prediction-What do you think Charlie wins?

Chapter 29: Before and After Chart-compare the four children going home from the beginning of the story to the end of the story.

Chapter 30: Write the next chapter about what will happen next. How is Charlie feeling right now? What will happen to the Bucket family?

After Reading-Why is this book called *Charlie and the Chocolate Factory?*

W	O	N	K	A

Note: All of the children are now gone except for Charlie. Let's think back to what happened that caused the children to leave.

Character Name	Cause	Effect
Augustus Gloop		
Veruca Salt		
Violet Beauregarde		
Mike Teavee		

Series Reading

- Frog and Toad series by Arnold Lobel
- Henry and Mudge series by Cynthia Rylant
- Junie B. Jones series by Barbara Park
- Ivy and Bean series by Annie Barrows
- EllRay Jake series by Sally Warner
- Two Mice travel series by Donna Dalton
- The Bad Guys series by Aaron Blabey
- The Ramona Books by Beverly Cleary
- The Henry Books by Beverly Cleary
- Diary of a Wimpy Kid Series by Jeff Kinney
- The Hatchet Series by Gary Paulsen
- The Shadow Children Series by Margaret Patterson Haddix
- The Fudge Books by Judy Blume
- The Chronicles of Narnia by C.S. Lewis
- A Series of Unfortunate Events by Lemony Snicket
- Little House Books by Laura Wilder
- Humphrey Series by Betty G. Birney
- Sisters Grimm Series by Michael Buckley
- Dork Diaries Series by Rachel Renee Russell
- Black Lagoon Series by Mike Thaler
- Horrible Harry Series by Suzy Kline

Communication with parents is essential in helping students achieve literacy success. I have never met a parent tell they did not want their child to learn how to read. However, not all parents know how to help their child become a better reader. In the final section of this book, you will find letters that that you can send home to parents that support literacy at home. The example below is the half sheet that I sent home at least three times a year with a new list of book titles that the family can check out at the library.

Tackle Reading by Kathryn Starke is a book with motivational and inspirational stories written with over 45 contributing writers. The popular educational resource helps parents promote reading at home all year long. I have had fathers who did not go to college themselves thank me for writing a book that they can read and understand to better help their children. When we build a strong connection between home and school with communication, we are truly creating a community of readers.

Dear Parents/Guardians,
        At this point in the year, your child _____
is reading at the following level:

below benchmark   on benchmark   above benchmark

Attached is a list of book titles that match your child's independent reading level. Thank you for encouraging nightly reading with a "just right" book.

Building background knowledge is the most important component that is needed to increase reading comprehension, which is the ultimate goal in reading. Sadly, it is also the first piece to either be removed from or not planned in a reading lesson. Our understanding of any subject is based on our own life experiences. Children with limited background experiences have a more difficult time relating to text or activating prior knowledge. Therefore, we need to find out what our students know and do not know and create a lesson accordingly.

When we ask students to make predictions before reading, they are telling us what they already know. When we ask them to make predictions during and after reading, they are showing us what knowledge or experience they have in life. Our students dictate what our lesson should look like. When we assume that they know nothing, we plan the best lesson. For example, if we are reading a book about a garden, I need to find out how many of my students have a fruit, vegetable, or flower garden at home or in their neighborhood. Then, we can plant a school garden or take a virtual tour of the White House Garden. After reading any text, I encourage my students to make a connection. The following pages support background knowledge instruction before, during, and after reading.

Possible Predictions

Book Title: _____

*Look at the title of the story. What do you predict will happen?

I predict _____

_____

_____

*Now, take a picture walk. What do you predict will happen?

I predict _____

_____

_____

Was your prediction confirmed? Yes or No? Explain.

_____

_____

_____

_____

Make a Connection: What does the story make you think about? _____

_____

_____

_____

_____

Name _____ Date _____

Book Title: _____

What does this story, text, or chapter remind you of?

What does this story, text, or chapter make you think of?

What is the "Science of Reading"?

If you have not already heard the term the "science of reading," you will begin to hear it more often. While it is a new phrase in education, it is not new information in literacy. The science of reading describes the five pillars of that are essential in the developmental reading process.

1. Phonological Awareness
2. Phonics
3. Vocabulary
4. Fluency
5. Comprehension

The first three pillars relate to working with words. While **phonological awareness** is usually implemented in primary classrooms, students who are labeled as English Language Learners, identified as a struggling reader, or requiring special educational services in reading may need additional work in phonological awareness. The oral practice of playing with words and sounds is the basis of early literacy.

Many educators also associate **phonics** with primary classrooms as well; however, phonics instruction spans from kindergarten to seventh grade. Phonics instruction explores the written sound-letter relationships in reading and writing. It ranges from letter sounds to word families to Latin and Greek roots and affixes. Children need a variety of experiences decoding (reading) and encoding (writing) phonics patterns.

A child's **vocabulary** is developed through conversation and reading. Therefore, a child who enters kindergarten without having been read to during their early years will already be significantly behind in understanding the meaning of commonly used words or phrases.

When a child reads with automaticity, smooth phrasing, accuracy, and a good reading rate, a child has **fluency**. Strong phonics skills, good decoding strategies, and an automaticity of word recognition are indicators that a child is a fluent reader.

When a child is a fluent reader, they are able to focus on **comprehension**, the understanding of text and the ultimate goal of reading. In the following sections, you will find a variety of lessons and activities to support word work, fluency, and comprehension at any grade level in your classroom. Each lesson can be implemented in small group, whole group, collaborative, or independent instructional experiences in K-5 classrooms.

Early Literacy and Phonological Awareness

Concept of word is a key predictor in a child's reading ability and literacy journey. When children do not have a concept of word in kindergarten, they are usually considered struggling readers in third grade. I always say that the strongest reading teachers should be in kindergarten and first grade where the foundations of reading are taught. Until administrators and educational leaders understand the importance of early literacy, we will continue to see the same results that were revealed by the 2019 National Assessment of Educational Progress (NAEP). Thirty-seven percent of fourth grade students in America read on grade level. This number falls to twenty-two percent when we are only looking at fourth grade students in low-income areas in America.

When we think about our students' background experiences, we must consider the fact that sixty-four percent of homes in low income areas do not have children's books. We may have children in our classrooms that have never been read to or even held a children's book. We also may have children that cannot read their name, recognize the letters in their name, or write their name. Therefore, our pre-K and kindergarten classrooms should be print-rich environments. Lower grade teachers should be encouraged to read picture books not only in language arts, but also in math, science, and social studies. Differentiated instruction should focus on the following early literacy skills: letters, sounds, rhyme, and concept of word.

When I see states and schools that promote developmentally appropriate kindergarten and first grade classrooms, I know they have a strong focus on literacy. Kindergarten and first grade classrooms should not have the same type of schedule or expectations as a third, fourth, or fifth grade classroom. I think back to one of my consulting visits at an exceptional elementary school in Charleston, South Carolina. This school, located in a low socioeconomic area, had children as young as three-years-old attend. I observed small groups of these preschool age children writing their names, reading books, learning the alphabet, using menus to play restaurant, and building with blocks.

These children attended pre-K to expand upon their knowledge in concept of print, letter recognition, and letter sounds. By the time these students arrived in kindergarten, they were ready to read. Elementary schools that house pre-kindergarten classrooms should create a professional learning community that closely aligns pre-kindergarten and kindergarten. When I visit schools, there is one questions I ask that many principals can't answer. *How many of your kindergarten students attended pre-k?* This is usually because there is not a system in place tracking the reading journey of these young learners. I encourage every school to determine an easy way to monitor this valuable information.

Kindergarten is still the first formal school experience for many children. When we understand this important fact, we begin to recognize the importance of implementing the same developmental practices and early literacy skills from preschool and pre-K classrooms into our kindergarten classrooms.

Sofia entered kindergarten as a non-English speaker who just moved to the United States from Mexico. I was the K-5 reading teacher at her school, so Sofia started working with me the second week of school. I knew enough Spanish to communicate with the five-year-old and quickly learned how much she already knew in her native language. I helped her understand the colors, days of the week, months of the year, food, and alphabet in English. Sofia is the best example of how being immersed in a classroom that promotes reading from day one. In addition to whole group literacy lessons and developmentally appropriate learning stations, Sofia had daily small group instruction with her classroom teacher and with me for the year. By the time Sofia was in third grade, she was one of the top readers in the grade level. When young readers receive the best instruction in early literacy, they become successful readers and life-long learners.

Each of the following activities in the early literacy and word work section can be used as an introductory lesson in whole group then placed into independent literacy stations.

- Concept of Print
- Concept of Word
- Syllables
- Rhyme
- Letter Recognition
- Letter Sound
- Word Families
- Word Structure

Phonological Awareness: Oral Instruction
*These activities can take place for 5-10 minutes daily in a whole group setting
*These are great ideas during K-2 transition time (lining up, dismissal, hallway engagement)

Syllable Segmentation-Count the number of syllables in concept words
Example: names, colors, animals, shapes, days, months, holidays, etc.

Rhyme-Recognize, differentiate, and produce words that rhyme
Activity 1: Matching pictures of rhyme pairs
Activity 2: Give a thumbs up or thumbs down if the word pair rhymes
Activity 3: Say the word hat. Ask student to provide as many words as they can that rhyme
with the word hat.

Alliteration-Recognize, differentiate, and produce words that share the same first letter sound
Activity 1: Give a thumbs up or thumbs down if the words have the same first letter sound
Activity 2: Teach and use tongue twisters. (Example: Baby bunnies bite bottles.)

Initial Sound Segmentation-Recognize, differentiate, and produce the initial sound of a word
Activity 1: Say the word mop. Ask students: what is the first sound that you hear? (*m*)
Activity 2: "There was an old lady who swallowed a P." (penny, pickle, pig, paper, etc.)
Activity 3: Play "I'm going to California and I'm going to take a _____." (ABC order)

Medial Sound Segmentation-Recognize, differentiate, and produce the medial sound of a word
Activity: Say the word mop. Ask students: what is the middle sound that you hear? (*o*)

Final Sound Segmentation-Recognize, differentiate, and produce the final sound of a word
Activity: Say the word mop. Ask students: what is the final sound that you hear? (*p*)

Phoneme Segmentation-Recognize, differentiate, and break apart each sound of a word
Activity 1: Say the word mop. Ask students to say each sound they hear in the word. (*m/o/p*)
Activity 2: Use sound boxes, beans, hand motions, walking, marching, or jump rope

Phoneme Blending-Recognize, differentiate, and put together each sound to make a word
Activity 1: Say the sounds (*m/o/p*). Ask students to say the word.
Activity 2: Use sound boxes

Phoneme Manipulation-Recognize, differentiate, and rearrange sounds to make a new word
Activity: Say the word mop. Change the *m* (sound) to a *t.* Ask students to say the word. (*top*)
Say the word top. Change the *o* (sound) to an a. Ask students to say the word (*tap*)
Say the word tap. Change the *p* (sound) to an *n*. Ask students to say the word (*tan*)

Name _____ Date _____

Concept of Print Checklist

Directions: Give each student a real book. Check each component the child can complete.

_____ I can identify the front book cover.   _____ I can identify the back book cover.

_____I can identify the author   _____I can identify the illustrator

_____ I can identify the title   _____ I can identify the spine

_____ I can read from left to right.   _____ I can read from top to bottom.
  (Note: Turn to a page in the book for them to point to where they start reading.)

Total: _____/6

Name _____ Date _____

Concept of Print Checklist

Directions: Give each student a real book. Check each component the child can complete.

_____ I can identify the front book cover.   _____ I can identify the back book cover.

_____I can identify the author   _____I can identify the illustrator

_____ I can identify the title   _____ I can identify the spine

_____ I can read from left to right.   _____ I can read from top to bottom.
  (Note: Turn to a page in the book for them to point to where they start reading.)

Total: _____/6

Rain, Rain Go Away

Come Again Another Day

Little _____ Wants to Play

Rain, Rain Go Away

Note: A child does not have a strong sense of concept of word if they cannot do all of the following tasks with a selected poem or text.

*Identify the number of words in each line
*Identify the number of spaces in each line
*Identify the number of letters in each word
*Identify the first and last letter in each word
*Identify words in isolation from the poem or text
*Fill in the missing word of a selected sentence from the poem or text
*Put the scrambled sentence in sequence

Objective:The student will be able to sort and distinguish between upper and lowercase letters. Directions: The students will use fine motor skills to practice cutting out the nine boxes below. The child will then create two piles, sorting the uppercase B's and the lowercase b's in the appropriate pile. (NOTE: Letters are printed differently in all kinds of text, so this is a visual memory, recognition, and letter discrimination activity.)

b	b	B
B	B	b
B	B	b

Teaching Letters and Sounds

1. Sing the alphabet, say the alphabet, and jump rope the alphabet.
2. Use an alphabet board to say each letter name and letter sound.
3. Read alphabet books. Students should put their thumb up when they hear a specific letter sound as determined by the teacher.
4. Go on alphabet hunts in books, poems, and around the room.
5. Name game: students should read and write their names. Provide each student with an envelope with their name cut up inside. They need to use these envelopes daily until they have successfully put their name in order at least three days in a row.
6. Use playdough, shaving cream, bingo markers, etc. to write letters.
7. Match uppercase letters to lowercase letters.
8. Put alphabet sticks or cards in order.
9. Match letter sounds to pictures.
10. Create a classroom sound board.
11. Use environmental print (signs, coupons, ads, etc.) to sort by letters.
12. Letter recognition and letter sound bingo.

Activity 1: Memory Tray Game
1. Place at least seven objects on a tray that begin or end with the same letter.
2. Give students at least 10 seconds for students to examine the tray.
3. Cover the tray with a towel so no children can see the objects.
4. Teacher asks the students, "What letter do all of the objects begin/end with?"
5. Students need to list the items aloud or draw a picture of the items.

Activity 2: "There Was an Old Lady Who Swallowed a *letter name*"
1. Determine the alphabet letter for the song.
2. Students brainstorm all of the objects that start with this letter to share.
3. Teacher leads class in the song. "There was an old lady who swallowed a P. She swallowed a penny, pebble, pickle, pig, pencil, poop, pumpkin, etc.
4. Teacher can write the list of words children states and/or students can draw the pictures of all of the items the old lady swallowed in her belly.

WE'VE GOT THE BEAT!

Directions: Identify the number of syllables in picture cards. Color the number of boxes to match the number of syllables in each word.

10				
9				
8				
7				
6				
5				
4				
3				
2				
1				
Number of Syllables	One (1)	Two (2)	Three (3)	Four (4)

Pat-A-Cake

Directions: Recite the Pat-A Cake nursery rhyme. When the line says "mark it with a "b" (or any other letter of the alphabet, the student should write the letter on a cake below.

Pat-a-cake, Pat-a-cake, baker's man,
Bake me a cake as fast as you can,
Pat it and prick it and mark it with a <u>letter name,</u>
And put it in the oven for <u>student name</u> and me.

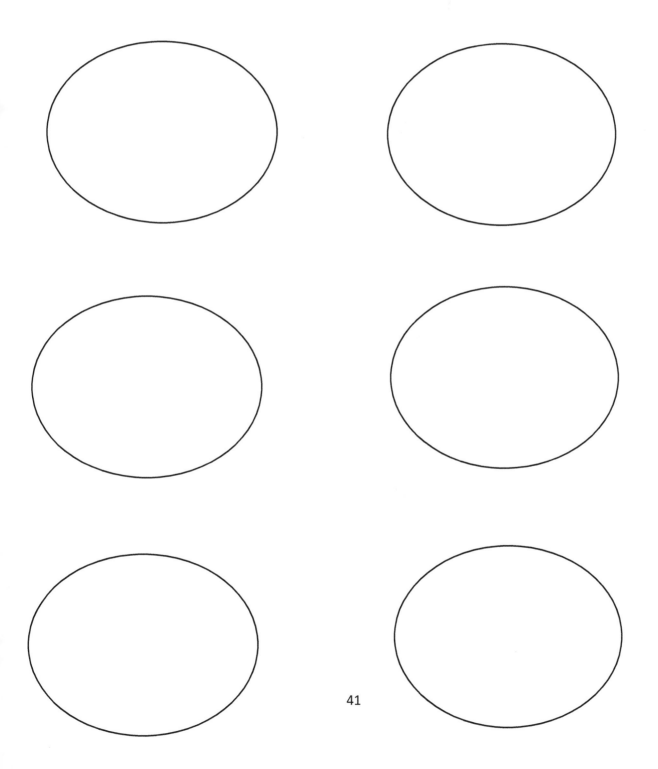

Word Work (Phonics/Sight Words)

Jerome entered my first-grade classroom standing tall at 5 feet 6 inches (I am 5'8"). The six-year-old possessed the interpersonal skills to engage with fifth graders and the reading knowledge of a kindergartner. He could read two words-*no* and his name. Jerome and I got along well because I gave him the space, support, praise, and redirection he needed to be successful in his new school community. I also gave him personalized reading instruction to help him achieve literacy success. When his mom and I met in November to discuss her son's progress, she told me a story I will never forget. She explained how Jerome went to basketball practice with the group of boys from his neighborhood and students in the previous school he attended. The boys asked him where he had been to which he confidently and proudly responded, "I go to a school that teaches you to read." What would Jerome say about your school? Children want to learn to read and they are looking for the teacher who is going to them. Will that be you?

Phonics is an essential component that must be present in classrooms. Many administrators and educators associate phonics with lower grades. Developmentally, however, a full understanding of phonics patterns and word structure range from preschool to seventh grade. Students need an equal balance of reading and writing to increase phonics knowledge. A child's reading and writing levels primarily depend on their understanding of phonics in the primary grades. I love visiting first grade classrooms during a writing time and guessing each child's instructional reading level based on their writing. I am usually correct, and love seeing the shock on the teachers' faces when I am. I would love to say it is a superhero talent I have, but it is simply because reading and writing is development. There is a particular sequence to teach phonics patterns, which are evident in a young reader's literacy journey. Often times, a child is a better reader than writer. I believe this is because we do not have a strong balance of decoding and encoding in primary classrooms. When we show children how reading and writing are connected through words, the developmental process of learning to read makes so much more sense. This section provides specific ideas and activities to implement phonics instruction in your classroom no matter what program you may be following.

Reading and Word Study Levels Correlation Chart

Guided Reading Level	DRA	Word Study Stage
A	1	Early Letter Name
B	2	Early Letter Name
C	3	Early-Mid Letter Name
D	4	Letter Name
E	6,8	Mid-Late Letter Name
F	10	Late Letter Name
G	12	Early Within Word
H	14	Early Within Word
I	16	Early Within Word
J	18	Within Word
K	20	Within Word
L	24	Mid-Late Within Word
M	28	Mid-Late Within Word
N	30	Late Within Word
O	34	Late Within Word
P	38	Early Syllable Juncture
Q, R, S	40	Syllable Juncture
T, U, V	50	Derivational Relations
W, X, Y	60	Derivational Relations
Z	70,80	Derivational Relations

*Adapted from University of Richmond School of Continuing Studies and Lindemann & Fowler

I   **R**   **E**   **A**

Dear Parents/Guardians,

      I am delighted to have the opportunity to work with your kindergarten child this year. In the beginning of the year, we will focus on our letter recognition and letter sounds that will help the students make words and sentences on their own. Your child's first project this year to be to complete a "letter lesson." Each child has selected a letter (either a consonant or vowel) from a hat and will be "teaching" their letter to the class. The bullet points below show exactly what the lesson should include. Please use them as a framework. Be as creative and original as possible.

> ➤ Show the uppercase and lowercase manuscript letter
>
> ➤ Provide a visual of an object that begins with the same letter   **N**
>
> ➤ Make up a silly sentence that uses at least 3 words that begin with that same letter

      The pictures of these items will be posted on our classroom soundboard so that the kindergarten students become alphabet experts. Thank you for your support.

Your child has selected the letter _____

Sincerely,

Your Kindergarten Teacher   **E**

PS: All of the letters around this page make a special word!   **G**

K   **N**   **R**   **T**

Introducing Phonics with Student Names

Directions: Provide the class roster of each student's first name in the form of a sort or list. Students should cut out each name to use in a phonics sort. Use a new feature or concept from the following list to observe and teach phonics features K-5. It can be a review or introductory lesson.

- Letters in my name/Letters NOT in my name
- Sort them by letter, pattern, blend, digraph, syllable, or length
- Play the name game (rhyme)
- Put them in ABC order
- Create the possessive of the name
- Vowels versus consonants
- Make new words out of them
- Compare and contrast the names
- Try all of this with the students' last names

ch	th
Charlie Bran**ch**	Ka**th**ryn An**th**ony **Th**alia
sh	**wh**
Shane Tani**sh**a	**Wh**itney

Tally the Beginning Sounds (Letter Hunt in Big Books or Classroom Library)

A
B
C
D
E
F
G
H
I
J
K
L
M
N
O
P
Q
R
S
T
U
V
W
X
Y
Z

Beginning Blends
(students should draw pictures of words that will help them learn the blends)

br	cr	dr	fr
gr	pr	tr	bl
cl	fl	gl	pl
sl	sn	sm	sk
sp	st	sw	tw

CH FOOD

I eat chicken.

I eat cheese.

I eat cheeseburgers.

I eat Chinese food.

I eat chili.

I eat chocolate.

Chomp, chomp, Chomp!

Compound Words: Cut out each word below and find its match to make a compound word. Glue the compound word together and draw a picture of the word.

Another Option: _____ + _____ =_____

                     hot   +   dog   =   hotdog

*Draw a picture of each of the three words

back	fire	brush	out
coat	rain	side	box
place	paint	pack	mail
sail	shell	boat	sea

Teaching Word Families

➢ **Use Nonsense Words**
- tup
- mip
- nop
- sak
- len

➢ **Create Word Ladders (use consonant and blend chart)**
  - **-ip**: dip, hip, lip, nip, rip, sip, tip, zip, chip, ship, whip, drip, clip, blip, quip, slip, trip, etc.

➢ **Use poems and songs to teach word families**

We are little pancakes,
Round and flat.
Stack us together
Just like that.
Add a pat of butter
On the top.
Then pour on the syrup
'Til we say "stop!"

➢ **Building Words:** How many 2 letter, 3 letter, 4 letter or more words can you make from the word *Thanksgiving* or the following letters?
(t, r, a, l, p, e, n)

Word Family Instruction

While it is important to provide differentiated word study instruction to match student's reading developmental needs, I find that teaching grade level appropriate whole group phonics lessons makes a huge difference in a child's literacy journey. Teaching word families in kindergarten, first, and second grade is the most effective way to do this. The introductory lesson should include books, poems, or hands-on activities to teach the word family. Then, students can work independently and in small groups throughout the week with activities that focus on the word family. I provide students with an alphabet chart and/or blend chart to support their writing. Accountability is essential in helping students become successful readers and writers. When I have finished teaching a word family or phonics pattern, I write it on an index card and add it to the phonics wall. Students are expected to read and write every word with this phonics pattern correctly.

Introductory and Whole Group Lessons

- Read a book or poem with a focus on the targeted word family
- Display big words to show students how to identify "hidden words" in decoding new words. Example: acrob**at**, m**ill**ion, **cap**tain
- Morning Message
- Dictated Sentences
- Use props, movement, or hands-on activities to teach the pattern
  -an: Host a pancake party. Make an "I Can" can.
  -ap: Apple sorting, tasting, and graphing
  -ad: Create feeling faces (mad, sad, glad, bad
  -ag: Fill a word bag of pictures that have the *ag* sound in it.
  -ack: Teach hand clap to *Miss Mary Mack*
  -ain: Put a train of letters or words in alphabetical order.
  -eg: Plan an egg hunt of words with the *eg* sound in it.
  -ig: Plan a pig day or teach the students a special jig.
  -op: Teach the bunny hop.
  -un: Read outside under the sun.
  -ch: Learn the Cha Cha to dance out *ch* words
  -sh: Tiptoe around the room sharing *sh* words

Independent and Literacy Station Word Work

- Sorts: pictures and words
- Decodable Books
- Word Hunts: poems, newspapers, magazines, books, etc.
- Sound Boxes
- Rhyming word ladders
- Poems
- Word Games
- Manipulatives: chalk, magnetic letters, stickers, stamps, etc.
- Writing activity
- Making Words
- Clues: Example-"This word rhymes with jet and starts with a v. It is the name of an animal doctor."
- Seasonal Word Families: turkey feathers, snowballs, hearts, etc.

Dear Parents/Guardians,

As you know, our goal this year is for each first grader to become an independent reader. The students are so proud to share their word sort bag and "take home" book with you again this week. We are still focused on the short a vowel sound and the word family *an*. Therefore, our first project this year will be the "I Can Can."

The assignment is to decorate an empty can with something your child **can** do exceptionally well. For example, your child may be great at playing a particular sport, riding a bike, or dancing. Maybe your child can read, write, draw, or tie his or her own shoe really well. Please allow your child to think about something he or she **can** do. Be creative!

Your child can also put something in the can that goes along with whatever skill they can do. The project will be due on _____. On this day, your child will share his or her "I Can Can" with the class. It will be a special way to review our newest word family while learning more about our new friends in school. Thank you!

Sincerely,

Directions: Read the short story and circle the words that have the short *a* vowel sound. On the back, sort them by word family.

That Cat!

Pat Cat has a red hat. Jan has a blue van. One day, Pat and his hat got on the van. The hat sat on Pat and on Bat and on Rat. Jan and Dan ran the van. The fan on the van was on, so the hat went off the van. Pat Cat said, "that hat!"

Draw what you think happens next.

Use the story to answer the following questions.

1. What color is the hat? _____

2. Who has a blue van? _____

3. Who had on the hat? _____

4. What made the hat go off the van? _____

Directions: Read the short story and circle the words that have the short *i* vowel sound. On the back, sort them by word family.

The Big Dig

The class went on a big dig. They found one wig. They found two figs. They found three pigs. They found a big pit. Erica had to sit. Zion had a fit. Piper had to quit. What did they see in the big pit?

Draw a picture of what you think they saw in the big pit.

Use the story to answer the following questions.

1. What was the first thing they found? _____

2. They found three _____.

3. What did Zion do? _____

4. Who wanted to quit? _____

5. Would you like to go on a dig? _____ Why or why not? _____

   _____

Sound Boxes

What's Missing?

d_____g   s_____n

f____sh   a____d

h____t   th____

Picture Words

m_____g

c_____t

b_____s

_____ ird

_____an

It's Magic e

**When you add an *e* to the end of CVC word, the short vowel becomes long, and the long vowel says its name.

Example: You can turn a tub into a tub**e** or a cub into a cub**e**

Directions: Choose two of the word pairs below to draw a picture of each word. On the back, make a list of as many additional word pairs that you can.

cap-cape   fir-fire   kit-kite   cub-cube   man-mane   pan-pane
tub-tube   van-vane   hug-huge   hop-hope   glob-globe

Magic *e* Hunt

a__e	e___e	i__e	o__e	u__e

Sight Words/High Frequency Words

A guided reading book that is labeled *C* or *D* usually has 75% of sight words or high frequency words in the text. Therefore, if a child has difficulty memorizing these words, they will not move out of the *C/D* range. What can we put in place to teach sight words? Firstly, we do not tell children to "sound out a word they do not know." This advice causes children to sound out sight words; if they do that, they will never correctly pronounce the words *what, where,* or *because.* Instead, we have to focus on ways for children to remember the order of particular letters or the word as a whole.

We can sing, step, clap, chant, or march them. Teach all of the forms of one word at one time. When you teach the word jump, teach them the plural, past tense, and present participle. Allow students to make their own flash cards for words they are personally missing. Encourage them to use two different colors to clearly identify the consonants and vowels in each word. On the back, ask them to draw a picture to match the meaning. For example, I would draw a picture of pizza for *like* because I really like pizza.

Remember when we talked about creating a classroom environment that promotes literacy and learning? A word wall was on the list. However, when I see an entire word wall displayed the first week of school, I know the resource is not being used correctly as a reading tool. The best way to use the word wall is to teach 3-4 new words a week using various activities listed below and add to the wall. Children are only expected to correctly read or write the words you have explicitly taught, which increases every single day.

- word wall

- personalized flash cards or word wall

- sight word bingo

- sight word memory/concentration

- pat the consonants, clap the vowels
  Example: like

- sight word hunt in books

- sight word sort by first letter or number of letters

- dictation

- sight word songs
  3 letter words: *Jingle Bells* (example: ran)
  4 letter words: *YMCA* (example: city)
  5 letter words: *BINGO* (example: where)
  6 letter words: *This Old Man* (example: school)
  7 letter words: *RESPECT* example: because)

- sight word groups-teach all of the forms of the sight word at the same time

  Example: help
        helps
        helped
        helping
        helper

  Example: jump
        jumps
        jumped
        jumping

Sight Word Sort by Number

Directions: Choose a sight word from the word wall or flash card pile. Count the number of letters in the word. Then, write the word under the correct number column.

one	two	three	four	five	six	seven

Helping Students Become Independent Readers

You have taught your students their sight words, phonics patterns, and strategies to become a more fluent reader. Now, you are sitting at the guided reading table and your students are struggling with decoding words. They get to an unknown word and either stare at you for help or make up a word based on its first letter. Why is this happening? First, ask yourself the following questions:

1. Do they know this sight word in isolation? If so, then they need to practice the sight word in text.
2. Do they know this word family in isolation? If so, then they need to be able to make a list using the alphabet, digraphs, and blends to create a list of its rhyming words.

Next, think about the particular strategies the students know to help them figure out an unknown word. They need to know that you will not always be there to tell them a word. They also need to know they have to tools to decode the unknown word themselves.

Previously Used Strategies

Look at the anchor chart below. Yes, there are some helpful tips for students when trying to decode an unknown word. However, there are too many steps or suggestions for them to think about during reading. The next page provides us with a few clear and concise strategies to support readers at any grade level and any reading level.

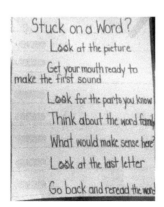

Effective Decoding Strategies

- When a child gets stuck on a word, there are **two** cueing systems teachers should use.

  - Is it a sight word, phonics-based word, or multisyllabic word? If it is a sight word tell the student that it is a sight word. This signals to the child's brain that this is a word he/she has already learned and should be on the word wall. I often snap when I say "sight word" signaling that automaticity of these words. When the word reappears in the text, I snap again, say "sight word" again, or say "it's the same word from the other page." Sometimes I will return to the previous page to see he/she recognizes or remembers the word.

  - We do not want to tell our students sound out a word. When they hear this prompt, they will often make each individual phoneme sound of every letter in the word. This practice makes it difficult for them to decode the unknown word. I recently watched a five-year-old "sound out" the word *when* to no avail. The sight word cue worked.

  - If it is a phonics-based or multisyllabic word, focus the student's attention on syllabication and hidden words within the unknown word. Syllabication is an early literacy skill that can easily be translated into decoding. Encourage children to draw lines between syllables, cut apart each syllable, or cover up chunks of the word to indicate each syllable in the word. Once the child has decoded the word correctly, he/she must always say the word again.

  - Consider writing new multisyllabic words on index cards and cutting apart for students to put back together. Can the students put the syllables in sequence?

  - For younger readers, encouraging children to identify "hidden words" within the larger unknown word. Once the child has decoded the word correctly, he/she must always say the word again.
    Example: acrob**at**, milli**on**aire, de**part**ment

Student Choice: Connecting Word Work to Writing
*using high frequency words, word study patterns, or vocabulary

1. Sentences
2. Story
3. Letter
4. Shopping List (Classification)
5. Silly Sentences (**T**ommy **r**an **u**nder **c**hocolate **k**isses. truck)
6. Lyrics
7. Pictures and Labels
8. Poems
9. Rhyming sentences, poems, and word list
10. Syllables
11. Handwriting-manuscript and cursive
12. Rap song
13. Memory/Concentration
14. Manipulatives: magnetic letters, chalk, stickers, stencils, etc.
15. Games: Scrabble, Bingo, Scattergories, etc.

Understanding Word Structure and Meaning: Prefixes

Name _____

-re=again, *-un*=not, *-dis*=do the opposite of, *-pre*=before, *-mis*=wrong

Directions: Use the prefixes above to help you understand the following questions and statements.

1. Rewrite the following sentence: A prefix is added to the beginning of a word.

   _____

   _____

2. What is a food that you dislike? _____

3. What happened when you misplaced your favorite shirt? _____

   _____

4. Have you ever had a misunderstanding with someone? _____ If so, what happened?

   _____

5. What is something that makes you unhappy? _____

6. What is your most unforgettable memory? _____

   _____

7. Tell me about something you think is unfair. _____

   _____

8. If you could disappear, where would you go? _____

9. What movie or show are you excited about watching after seeing the preview?

   _____

10. Draw a quick sketch of what you think it looked like in prehistoric times.

Suffix: *ly*

You're wearing your squeaky shoes,
And right there taking a snooze
Is a tiger, so how do you walk by?
Silently, silently, silent**ly**

You're a secret agent man
Who's after a secret plan.
How do you act so they don't know you're a spy?
Normally, normally, normal**ly**

At an eating contest you boast
That you can eat the most.
How do you down your fiftieth piece of pie?
Eagerly, eagerly, eager**ly**

In the public library
You fall and hurt your knee.
But the sign says QUIET PLEASE, so how do you cry?
Quietly, quietly, quiet**ly**

As you walk along the street
A porcupine is who you meet.
How do you shake his hand when he says hello?
Carefully, carefully, careful**ly**

You enter a very dark room,
And sitting there in the gloom is Dracula.
How you say goodbye?
Immediately, immediately, immediate**ly**
Bye, bye!

Created by Kathryn Starke

Note: A suffix is a tiny part that is added to the end of a base word to change the meaning. Cover up the *-ly* in the words below to determine if it is used as a suffix or is the part of a word.

simply   butterfly

family   reply

silly   slowly

quickly   freely

Willy   secretly

Suffix Schedule

Name _____

Directions: Below is a schedule of words that contain a suffix. A suffix comes at the end of a base word and changes its meaning. Answer the questions below to learn more about the meanings.

larger- Which is larger? a fox or a horse	**smaller-** Which is smaller? a mouse or a kitten	**longest-** What chore at home takes the longest to do?	**beautiful-** What is something that is considered beautiful to you?	**careless-** If a teacher says you made a careless mistake in your work, what does that mean?
teacher- Who is your favorite teacher of all time?	**wonderful –** How do you feel when someone says you did a wonderful job on your project?	**tallest-** Who is the tallest person is your family?	**colorful-** What is the most colorful thing you own?	**baker-** If you were a baker, what would your special treat be?
motionless- If you are motionless, what are you doing?	**fastest-** Who is the fastest basketball player in the league?	**lighter-** What is lighter? a feather or a pencil	**reporter-** What is one story you would tell if you were a reporter?	**lovely-** Who is someone that is lovely in your eyes?

***Let's Review: Possessives, Contractions, and Plurals

Name _

Use the picture above to help understand these language arts terms.

1. **Zoey's** computer is new. (Zoey' s=**possessive**= something that belongs to someone. Who does the computer belong to? Zoey)

2.The cat **can't** play with the computer. (can't=**contraction**=a shortcut version of two words; can' t=cannot)

3.Zoey is wearing a skirt with a lot of **polka dots.** (polka dots=**plural**=more than one of something)

*Now, read the sentences below and circle the **possessive.**

1.The man's car is fast and furious.
2.The baker's donuts are the best in town!

*Now, read the sentences below and circle the **contraction.**

1. I wouldn't do that if I were you.
2. I didn't know we had homework last night.

*Now, read the sentences below and circle the **plural.**
1. My socks are soaking wet!
2. I would like extra cherries on top, please.

Contractions

Directions: Match the contraction to the words it correctly replaces.
Extension: Distribute a card for each student for them to find their partner.

do not	are not	it is	I am
didn't	she will	who's	who is
I'm	is not	don't	she'll
isn't	it's	did not	aren't

Name _____ Date _____

Who owns what?

Example: the racecar of Dale   <u>Dale's racecar</u>

Use the statements below and make it into a possessive!

1. the skirt of Miss Starke _____

2. the basketball of Mr. Graham _____

3. the sweater of Mrs. Johnson _____

4. the office of the principal _____

5. the movie of Lizzie _____

6. the computer of Jake _____

7. the letter of Dr. Hall _____

8. the playlist of Annie _____

9. the baseball cap of the team _____

10. the boat of the captain _____

***Now make your own!

Macaroni Possessives

Name _____

Directions: Read each sentence below looking for <u>possessives</u> (when something belongs to somebody). When you find one, place the macaroni noodle (the apostrophe) in the proper place.
**Don't be fooled by contractions, plurals, or compound words!

1. Miss Starkes favorite food is pizza.

2. Don't forget to get your moms signature on the form.

3. I cannot wait to win my coachs ticket to the baseball game.

4. The gardeners flowers are beautiful this time of year.

5. The singers albums are always on the Billboard charts.

6. Isn't that your dads car?

The Plural Girls

Name _____

Directions: Use the choices of endings below to change the singular noun into a plural noun.

Add s   Add es   Change y to i
                                                   then add es

1. day _____
2. dish _____
3. baby _____
4. watch _____
5. rose _____
6. pony _____
7. song _____
8. mountain _____
9. city _____
10. peach _____
11. monkey _____
12. country _____
13. french fry _____
14. dress _____

Draw and spell one strawberry and more than one strawberry.

Singular/Plural Nouns: Cut out each word below and sort into two columns.

boy	paper
girls	books
cup	toys
cars	bus
lunch	school
pencils	games

Contractions, Possessives, and Plurals...Oh my!!

Name _____

Directions: Choose 3 crayon colors. Choose one color to circle all of the contractions. Choose the next color to circle all of the possessives. Choose the final color to circle all of the plurals. Don't let the apostrophe fool you!

hasn't	calendars	wasn't
classmates	they're	Mr. Smith's
students	who's	celebrations
geese	Americans	teacher's
cousins	children	berries
girls'	couldn't	Charlie's
Maggie's	she's	won't
isn't	teachers	students'

Fairy Tale Homophones

Directions: Read each sentence below. Circle any homophone that is used incorrectly. Write the correct homophone on the line.

1. The prince kissed Sleeping Beautify and asked her if she wood merry him.

   _____

2. The cruel animals maid fun of the Ugly Duckling.

   _____

3. Deer Cinderella went to the ball with the help of her ferry godmother.

   _____

4. Fare Rapunzel let down her long, golden hare.

   _____

5. The which tried to fatten up Hansel and Gretel two put sum meet on there bones.

   _____

6. The wolf blue down the houses for the first too pigs.

   _____

7. The Emperor was to vane two admit he could knot sea his new clothes.

   _____

Once Upon
A Time...

Double Agent Words

Directions: Some words have more than one meaning. Use the word bank below to select the "one word" that makes sense in both sentences.

saw	park	can	bark	ring

1. Where did you _____ the car?
   Let's go play at the _____ this afternoon.

2. The lady is wearing a huge _____.
   Did you hear my phone _____?

3. I _____ a bird sitting on the stoop.
   I need a _____ to build the bench.

4. Would you open this _____ of soup for me?
   I _____ write my name perfectly.

5. The _____ of the tree is rough.
   That dog has very, loud _____.

   **Your turn. Can you think of a word that has two different meanings?
   Write the sentence pair below.

Fluency

Fluency: Practice Makes Perfect

- Guided Reading Books
- Classroom library (leveled books, genre study, author study, etc.)
- School library visit (choice book of interest)
- Big Books
- Poetry
- Decodable Books
- Partner Reading
- Listening Stations
- Reader's Theater
- SQUIRT/Independent Reading

When a reader has the automaticity of words, a smooth phrasing, accuracy, and an appropriate rate, a child has **fluency** in reading. Children only become fluent readers by reading often. I compare it to playing an instrument or sport; you get better the more you do it. (This is why I spent a large amount of this book on the power of motivation and engagement. I want children to love reading so they become great readers.) When children have strong word attack skills of phonics patterns and sight words, they have better fluency. Teaching fluency sometimes differs by grade level and reading level, but the end goal remains the same. When children are fluent readers, comprehension can be addressed.

All Classrooms:
-Independent Reading (SQUIRT: **S**uper **Q**uiet **U**ninterrupted **I**ndependent **R**eading **T**ime)
-Grade level appropriate reader's theater (for groups of students, not whole group)
-Partner Reading (high/low; upper grade/lower grade)
-Repeated Reading

K-1 Classrooms:
-Focus on punctuation (stopping and starting)
-Focus on expression (see reading behavior strips on next page)
-Word Wall Phrases/Common Phrases (Example: up or down, over the rainbow, etc.)
-Big Books
-Poetry
-Choral Reading (read poems or specific parts of a text in unison (altogether)
-Echo Reading (teacher reads a line then students repeat the line)
-Listening Station

Read like a …
*Students draw a card or popsicle stick from a cup to practice reading like a _____.

Read like a robot.
Read like a giant.
Read like a baby.
Read like a cheerleader.
Read like a speed demon.
Read like a mouse.
Read like a monster.
Read like a great reader.

Reading is a developmental process for children between the ages of five and eight or kindergarten through third grade. Usually when students have an automaticity of sight words and phonic based words, fluency is present in reading. Research suggests that a child with strong fluency will have better comprehension. However, we have all seen students with excellent fluency and poor comprehension skills. We have also seen students with poor fluency and excellent comprehension skills.

Fluency is only administered through oral reading assessments or running records. It is often the sole component that holds a child back on a particular instructional level. Think about the student who is naturally in slow motion. He or she walks slowly, takes forever to unpack in the morning, and is the last one to finish lunch. Often times, this child will read "word by word." The previous activities will help every student improve their reading fluency in grades K-5.

In fourth and fifth grade, many children only struggle with fluency. Therefore, I will use fluency passages or specific pages of text as repeated readings to focus solely on fluency. Each year as a reading specialist, I would identify at least ten students in fifth grade who were documented on third grade reading level based on diagnostic reading tools. The only factor that kept them at the third-grade reading level was fluency. I would pick them up for a daily group from the beginning of the school year and tell them they would only be with me for the first semester. I knew that by the end of a few months, these students could be on a fifth-grade reading level after practicing fluency each day. Here are the steps that I used each week.

Day One:
1. Introduce a reading passage or specific pages of text that match their guided reading instructional level.
2. Tell the students their "words per minute" (wpm) goal for this particular text. Use the chart on the following page to provide the number or range that matches the students' grade level.
3. Instruct students to read aloud the provided passage until you say stop. You will time the students for one minute. The students can spread out around the guided reading table.
4. When the timer goes off after one minute, tell the students to put their finger on the last word they read and mark it with a star. Then instruct them to count the number of words they read in one minute.
5. Show the students how to graph their words per minute on a bar graph noting the date at the bottom of that column.
6. Celebrate readers who met the wpm goal. Explain to all readers what the goal is and how close they are to it.

Day Two:
1. Students can reread the passage on their own anywhere around the room.
2. Call students individually to read the passage to you for one minute. Take anecdotal notes documenting any errors during reading. After reading, point out the errors and teach any unknown words.

3. Instruct students to count the words they read <u>correctly</u> per minute and graph.
4. Celebrate readers who met the wpm goal. Explain to all readers what the goal is and how close they are to it.

Day Three:
1. Students can reread the passage on their own anywhere around the room.
2. Call students individually to read the passage to you for one minute. Take anecdotal notes documenting any errors during reading. After reading, point out the errors and teach any unknown words.
3. Instruct students to count the words they read <u>correctly</u> per minute and graph.
4. Celebrate readers who met the wpm goal. Explain to all readers what the goal is and how close they are to it.

After Day Three/Three Days of Repeated Reading:
- If the students have all met the wpm goal, choose a new text (same instructional reading level) to begin the three-day process again. Consider a different genre from previous text. After two different text readings, increase the instructional reading level of text for the next session following the grade level wpm guidelines.
- If the students have not met the wpm goal, add the same process for the fourth day then send the text home to practice. Begin a new text (same instructional reading level and same genre) the next day or next class.

On the pages that follow, you will see the grade level wpm chart, the teacher's recording sheet, and a blank bar graph. There is also a step by step guide of how to turn a text or passage into a reader's theater script to help improve fluency at any grade level.

AUTOMATICITY:

Grade	Fall	Winter	Spring
1	5	25	50-60 wcpm*
2	53	78	84-94
3	79	93	104-114
4	99	112	98-118
5	105	118	118-128
6	115	132	135-145
7	147	158	157-167
8	156	167	166-171

*words correct per minute

Procedure: Ask the student to read orally for one minute from grade-level curriculum material.

Scoring: Count the number of words read correctly in one minute (include self-corrections)

Analysis and Interpretation: 99% Correct: Independent Level Reading
95% Correct: Instructional Level Reading
90% Correct: Frustration Level Reading

Adapted from: Hasbrouck, J. E. & Tindal, G. (1992). Curriculum-based oral reading fluency forms for students in Grades 2 through 5. Teaching Exceptional Children, (Spring), 41-44. And Howe, K. B. & Shinn, M. M. (2001). Standard reading assessment passages (RAPS) for use in general outcome measurements: A manual describing development and technical features. Eden Prairie, MN: Edformations.

Fluency Check: 3rd Grade (WMP)

Grade 3	Early	Middle	Late
Expected:	79	93	104-114

Student	Date	GR Level	WPM

Fluency Check: 4th Grade (WMP)

Grade 4	Early	Middle	Late
Expected:	99	112	98-118

Student	Date	GR Level	WPM

Fluency Check: 5th Grade (WMP)

Grade 5	Early	Middle	Late
Expected:	105	118	118-128

Student	Date	GR Level	WPM

My Words Per Minute Graph

Name _____ Grade _____

Goal: _____

100									
95									
90									
85									
80									
75									
70									
65									
60									
55									
50									
45									
40									
35									
30									
25									
20									
15									
10									
5									

Date(s) of Each Day of Timed Reading (words in isolation or in text)

How to Turn a Book into Reader's Theater

1. Choose a book that matches the instructional level of your reading group.
2. Make a list of the main characters from the book.
3. Use the character dialogue in the book to write lines.
4. Use the text of background information and action to write lines for the narrator.
5. Write the lines in sequence to match the book.

Example: DRA 8/GR Level E adapted from *Late for School*

Narrator: Elephant ran by the firehouse and saw Lion.
Elephant: Why are you playing? We are late for school today!
Lion: Go away!
Narrator: Then Elephant ran by the playground and saw Mouse.

Vocabulary

Studies suggest that children who live in poverty grow up hearing at least four million fewer words by the age of three. This suggests that even some of our kindergarten students are entering school significantly behind their peers in language. Our **vocabulary** develops through reading, speaking, and listening. What words do you use on a regular basis with your students? Do you say *rules* or *expectations*? Do you say *schedule* or *routine*? Do you say *playground* or *recess*? When we expose children to a variety of words through conversation and read aloud experiences, their vocabulary increases. We can never predict what vocabulary words children do not know; it very much depends on their background knowledge and experiences. I remember one student who was labeled an English Language Learner did not know the word *pitcher*; his mom always used the word *bottle*. He may have never seen a *pitcher* before.

I encourage teachers to always discuss the pronunciation and meaning of words in text titles. I recall a third-grade class reading an article entitled *Rhino Rescue* to identify the main idea of the nonfiction text. None of the children could read the word *rescue*, so they had difficulty explaining the main idea. I also encourage teachers to select three words prior to reading any text and use the activities that follow daily to help children with increasing and expanding their vocabulary. When children are reading independently, encourage them to circle or write down the unknown words. It can be a word they can not pronounce or a word they can pronounce but do not know the meaning. This information helps teachers develop more appropriate lessons to increase understanding.

While vocabulary is best taught through text or context in any subject, we know that not every book will teach words that the average fourth grader should know. Therefore, I have added five- minute daily vocabulary lessons in classroom for third grade and above. In this section, you will find lessons, activities, and support to help your students increase their vocabulary.

Fancy Words with *Fancy Nancy*

Nancy's Word Choice	My Word Choice
Ecstatic	
Ensemble	
Posh	
Spectacular	
Unique	
Exquisite	
Gorgeous	
Furious	
Extraordinary	

*Lesson to be used to teach synonyms using the book *Fancy Nancy* by Jane O'Connor

Synonym Memory

friend	arithmetic	close
anthology	buddy	create
wiggle	hallway	desire
corridor	setting	sequence
want	chilly	math
stare	order	near
freezing	gaze	place

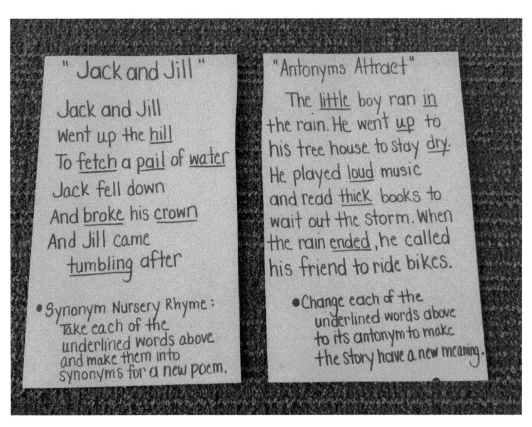

> **"Jack and Jill"**
>
> Jack and Jill
> Went up the <u>hill</u>
> To <u>fetch</u> a <u>pail</u> of <u>water</u>
> Jack fell down
> And <u>broke</u> his <u>crown</u>
> And Jill came
>   <u>tumbling</u> after
>
> • Synonym Nursery Rhyme:
>   Take each of the
>   underlined words above
>   and make them into
>   synonyms for a new poem.

> **"Antonyms Attract"**
>
> The <u>little</u> boy ran <u>in</u>
> the rain. He went <u>up</u> to
> his tree house to stay <u>dry</u>.
> He played <u>loud</u> music
> and read <u>thick</u> books to
> wait out the storm. When
> the rain <u>ended</u>, he called
> his friend to ride bikes.
>
> • Change each of the
>   underlined words above
>   to its antonym to make
>   the story have a new meaning.

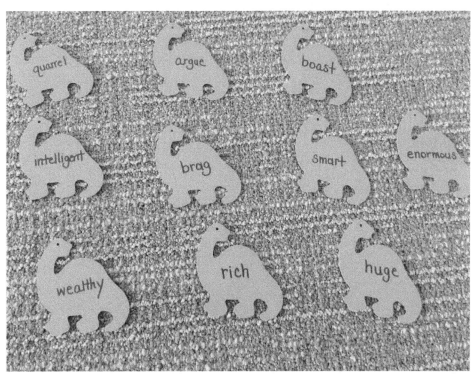

(thesaurus: a book of synonyms: "The saurus is looking for words that are the same!")

SAME WORD SAMMY

Sammy always likes to say the same thing over and over again. His teacher showed him how to choose a <u>synonym</u> to make his stories more interesting. Help Sammy find <u>synonyms</u> for the words below. Make a new word list below. (Group work suggested for this activity.)

1. delicious

2. happy

3. noise

4. surprised

5. cold

Introducing Vocabulary

1. Listen and Synonym Share

2. Guess the Covered Word (Ex: My mother works as a <u>waitress</u> in the Blue Tile Diner.)

3. Picture Walk and Story Board

4. Predictable Page: (Ex: coin jar, saving, bargain, fire, furniture, neighborhood, replace, purchase, delivery)

V is for...

vocabulary

These four introductory lessons can be used with any text at any grade level in either whole group or small group. The above examples are all associated with the book *A Chair for my Mother* by Vera B. Williams.

1. **Listen and Synonym Share**: Select three words from the text and write on the board or chart paper for children to see. Say each word and ask the students to repeat it after you. Instruct them to <u>listen</u> to each word while you are reading to them and ask them to either put their thumbs up or signal to you when they hear the word. When you see the signal, stop at the end of that sentence, and ask students to give you words that mean the same or something similar to this unknown word. You are creating an oral list of <u>synonyms</u>.
   Example: bargain-"As I read, I want you to listen for the word *bargain*. Put your thumb up as soon as you hear it." (Thumbs up) "Okay, *bargain*. Let me read that sentence again. What are some words that mean the same as *bargain* in this sentence?" Call on students. You are welcome to write them as well for students to see and read. Examples of words may include *deal, steal, savings, price*, etc. One of my students said *hook up*, which is a similar term to the word *bargain*. The goal is for the students to understand the meaning of the word based on their own vocabulary.
   Extension of Activity in Independent Work/Stations

bargain-Write meaning in own words	Picture of the word
List of Synonyms	List of Antonyms

2. **Guess the Covered Word:** This activity is ideal to do before reading with three preselected words from the text. It uses student phonics knowledge and context clues to determine the missing word.
   Example: My mom works as a _____ in the Blue Tile Diner.
   My mom works as a w_____ in the Blue Tile Diner.
   My mom works as a wait____in the Blue Tile Diner
   My mom works as a waitress in the Blue Tile Diner.

3. **Picture Walk and Story Board:** We all do a great job of incorporating a picture walk before reading at the guided reading/small group table. This activity allows you to use your student's vocabulary knowledge to support their decoding and reading skills. Listen to the words you use when telling you about the story and write them on a white board or piece of construction paper. This story board will be used for two days during guided reading.
   Example: The fiction story is about a bear family going fishing. List of words orally stated by students: bear, cub, fishing, trout, lake, stream, fishing rod, worms, etc.

   Write the list of words they say that appear in the text. More often than not, the vocabulary will match. At the end of the picture walk, instruct students to look at the story board and read the word list with you. (Either chorally or as an echo read depending on your students' age and reading level.) Keep the story board available for students to refer to when reading and find themselves "stuck" on a word. The reference board will often trigger their memory to figure out the word on their own. The next day, chorally read the words on the story board before reading then put the story board out of eyesight. You may see children look for it to help them because they remember seeing it before. Only use the board if absolutely necessary. These new words will soon become part of their reading vocabulary. Sometimes I display the story boards around the room with the title and/or cover illustration clearly documented.

4. **Predictable Page:** This activity is a great activity, especially for older students and higher readers. You can either have the students echo read the words with you, read them to you, or silently read them. The students are to use both their word and background knowledge to identify the main idea or theme of the text. Note that some of the words are actually in the text and some are not.
   Example: innovation, inventor, solution, technology, invention, world renowned
   Students may predict this book will be about an inventor, an invention, or a famous scientist.

GUESS THE COVERED WORD
Using the children's book
Dandelion by Don Freeman

1. On a sunny <u>Saturday</u> morning, Dandelion woke up, <u>stretched,</u> and yawned and jumped out of bed.

2. After doing his daily <u>exercises</u> Dandelion looked out of the window.

3. Dandelion thought he really should wear something more <u>elegant</u> than a sweater to the party.

4. A <u>bouquet</u> of dandelions would be perfect.

CLUE GYM

Detective Name(s)_____

Directions: Read the clues below. You are to figure out what the bold-faced word means using clue words in the sentence. Circle or highlight the clue words that help you. Once you know what the word means then you can figure out the location described in the actual clue.

On your CLUE GYM game board, write the bold-faced word on the line in the correct location box. To complete your game board, you must illustrate a little picture to show what the word means. Good luck!!!!

Clue:

1. We read the article in the daily **gazette** that said to bring our rackets here for match.
2. The player decided to **intercept** and make a touchdown here.
3. He had to **guard** the other team member, so he could not make a three pointer here.
4. We noticed that tiny white balls were **scattered** all over this green location.
5. The coach began to **scold** a player for using his hands on the ball and another player at this location.
6. The dark alleys in this place started to **illuminate** around the pins.
7. The **monsoon** of wind and rain damaged the bases which caused this location to cancel the game.
8. The **superior** player always scored points when she served the ball in this location.

Football Field

Bowling Alley

Tennis Court

Basketball Court

Golf Course

Soccer Field

Volleyball Court

Baseball Field

Daily Vocabulary Instruction

The next three pages provide a school year of vocabulary words that are most commonly seen on standardized tests in third, fourth, and fifth grade. Many of these words will not be seen by children if they are reading below grade level. Therefore, it is up to educators to expose them to new words. Five minutes a day helps increase word knowledge in pronunciation and meaning. We do not use dictionaries and do not give assessments. We use conversation and real-life experiences to add more words to our personal word bank.

Monday: Students decode the unknown words by cutting words apart through syllabication or identifying the hidden words. Once the words are properly pronounced, I ask the following questions. *Have you ever heard this word before? How? What does it mean?*

Tuesday: Students read each word and provide a definition in their own words.

Wednesday: Students use the words in oral sentences, questions, or quick conversation.

Thursday: Put students in groups to create a list of synonyms for their assigned word.

Friday: Create a quick pencil sketch of the meaning of the word.

Third Grade Vocabulary

Week 1: alone, suppose, certain, design
Week 2: amount, passenger, developed, several
Week 3: angle, direct, interesting, sudden
Week 4: appear, captain, discovered, supply
Week 5: century, electric, equivalent, search
Week 6: coast, enjoy, ache, figure
Week 7: consider, exactly, famous, annual
Week 8: consonant, expression, factors, bitter
Week 9: guess, increase, deny, fasten
Week 10: indicate, language, material, factual
Week 11: method, natural process, general
Week 12: moment, provide, pleasure, imagine
Week 13: raised, section, valuable, pioneer
Week 14: rather, separate, pupil, harvest
Week 15: receive, suggested, tender, blur
Week 16: region, suppose, honor, sincere
Week 17: remain, similarity, represent, average
Week 18: result, truthful, careless, phrase
Week 19: represent, experience, manage, deserve
Week 20: surround, foreign, error, indeed
Week 21: mention, disapprove, refund, sample
Week 22: struggle, modern, select, program
Week 23: solve, sense, tantrum, contrast
Week 24: transmit, balance, splurge, dainty
Week 25: dispute, decay, approach, steady
Week 26: loyal, awkward, layer, gnawing
Week 27: flawless, beware, adore, worthy
Week 28: aware, squabble, dozen, rehearse
Week 29: despair, earnest, journey, council
Week 30: local, shimmer, hollow, solitary
Week 31: mission, central, describe, settle
Week 32: sequel, nephew, create, conceited

Fourth Grade Vocabulary

Week 1: million, desert, seldom, drawer
Week 2: dessert, northern, accelerate, cavern
Week 3: stood, chase, separate, control
Week 4: shook, awhile, sour, promise
Week 5: cheap, reason, although, lean
Week 6: pleasure, bathe, company, whom
Week 7: nickel, pour, object, perhaps
Week 8: known, couple, interesting, arithmetic
Week 9: declare, glisten, exhaust, glance
Week 10: capture, wit, cling, valid
Week 11: brilliant, amateur, swift, gloomy
Week 12: arch, plunge, admirable, convince
Week 13: precious, harsh, coward, grant
Week 14: shallow, yearn, struggle, sensitive
Week 15: exclaim, fierce, observe, disturb
Week 16: shatter, superb, unite, clasp
Week 17: insist, border, pierce, clever
Week 18: rare, journey, accuse, imitate
Week 19: depart, triumph, remote, wisdom
Week 20: delicate, prompt, honor, brief
Week 21: compete, timid, reflex, conquer
Week 22: decay, intimidated, actual, fury
Week 23: ability, brink, approach, consider
Week 24: sufficient, glory, avoid, sergeant
Week 25: distant, magnificent, intend, revive
Week 26: previously, glide, dreary, wreckage
Week 27: origin, audible, meek, vibrant
Week 28: stout, opponent, authentic, modest
Week 29: scorn, clarify, woe, formal
Week 30: barrier, abundant, inquire, penalize
Week 31: union, necessary, adequate, doubtful
Week 32: wound, trophy, casual, coarse

Fifth Grade Vocabulary

Week 1: abolish, banquet, cautiously, debate
Week 2: edible, gigantic, hazy, identical, suspend
Week 3: miniature, narrator, oasis, pedestrian
Week 4: reassure, saunter, visible, wilderness
Week 5: withdraw, visual, taunt, seldom, apparent
Week 6: absurd, beverage, challenge, decline, synonym
Week 7: endanger, guardian, petrify, illuminate
Week 8: minor, navigate, obsolete, suffocate
Week 9: reign, senseless, thrifty, vivid, approximate
Week 10: tropical, slither, reliable, abuse, aroma
Week 11: access, bland, character, detect, assume
Week 12: escalate, immense, mischief, negative
Week 13: nonchalant, occasion, portable, reliable
Week 14: resemble, sluggish, translate, accomplish
Week 15: achievement, blizzard, companion, dictate
Week 16: exasperate, blizzard, companion, dictate
Week 17: overthrow, preserve, retain, soar, astound
Week 18: solitary, aggressive, budge, crave, available
Week 19: document, exert, independent, moral, course
Week 20: purchase, retire, solo, alternate, courteous
Week 21: altitude, bungle, compassion, duplicate
Week 22: exhibit, industrious, myth, route, avalanche
Week 23: sparse, intense, compensate, antagonist
Week 24: compose, intercept, spurt, strategy
Week 25: concept, anxious, suffix, confident

*3rd, 4th, and 5th grade word list compiled from National Reading Panel's list of most used words in standardized tests

Name _____

miscellaneous: adjective, consisting of a various kind or qualities; a collection of unrelated objects
Example: The miscellaneous drawer holds glue, notepads, stickers, and candy.

Directions: After reading *Miss Alaineus: A Vocabulary Disaster* **by Debra Frasier, read each sentence below. Determine the meaning of the underlined words by using the clues in the sentence. Then, draw a picture of a "Miss" (just like the book) to help you remember what the word means.**

1. The lady was <u>misinformed</u> about the party and showed up on the wrong day.

2. I have seemed to <u>misplace</u> my keys yet again in this house.

3. Did you make a <u>mistake</u> on your writing assignment?

4. Use your dictionary so you do not <u>misspell</u> any words.

5. <u>Misery</u> loves company because no one wants to be unhappy alone.

Character Trait Vocabulary Match

The **admirable** behavior of the young boy showed why he was class president.	She was clearly **appreciative** for her presents when she said thank you to everyone.
The **carefree** girl ran around the playground smiling and playing with every classmate.	The **demanding** teacher gave five hours of homework each night.
I asked my friend to pick her favorite kind of pizza, and she was too **indecisive** to come up with one.	Nobody likes the **egotistical** man because he acts like he's so great.
The **irritable** boy complained and whined during the entire movie.	We were so impressed by the very talented and **modest** violinist.
The **persistent** party planner called her guests repeatedly to see who would attend the event.	I knew the boy would be punished because he was so **rambunctious** during the assembly.
The **spiteful** teenager didn't give the phone message to her best friend.	The teacher was very **tolerant** of the child's negative behavior.
It was so nice to tell my sad story to a **sympathetic** teacher.	The **inquisitive** student asked tons of questions to the guest speaker.

praiseworthy Jackie Robinson	**rowdy** David from *No David*
hateful Cinderella's evil stepsisters	**understanding** Martin Luther King, Jr.
caring Snow White	**curious** Curious George
grateful birthday girl	**shy** Scaredy Squirrel

happy-go-lucky	**requesting**
Amelia Bedilia	mouse from *If You Give a Mouse a Cookie*
wishy-washy	**conceited**
Junie B. Jones	emperor from *The Emperor's New Clothes*
cranky	**determined**
screaming baby	Nancy Drew, detective

Clip art from pdclipart.org and wpclipart.com

Comprehension

Comprehension Strategies in Action

Comprehension is the ultimate goal of reading. When students have a strong phonics background and fluency, they can focus on reading comprehension. When we teach comprehension, it is important to remember not to teach a story, but rather to teach the strategies and skills of any story. Reading strategies should be used in any text in any genre at any grade level. Reading skills are more specific and should be taught with a text that best supports the skill. For example, you cannot teach compare and contrast if you do not have more than one character or setting in a text.

It is also imperative that children are learning comprehension strategies and skills at their grade level, independent reading level, and instructional reading level. While students may be unable to complete a cause and effect chart on grade level material, they may be successful using the same chart at their independent reading level or instructional reading level with teacher support. When this happens, the concept is not the issue, the readability of the text is the challenge. Therefore, we need to provide a number of opportunities with the same skill or strategy in a variety of text levels. At the end of a lesson or unit, consider using an exit ticket (the same question format or example) in whole group, small group, and independent reading time to assess comprehension.

While we model and scaffold instruction using grade level text for students, we continue to increase the difficulty of text in guided reading to lessen the reading gap. A "strategies and skills" chart is provided on the next page for reference. This section also includes graphic organizers and lessons that allow children to think about their reading. Consider adding a visual like a Magic 8 ball when teaching predictions. We understand that students should be able to comprehend any genre. Beginning in the third grade, the first genre of the school year I like to introduce is mystery. Strategies like inference and drawing conclusions, which are so difficult for students, are easily applied when reading mysteries. Once students have practiced being a reading detective and using these higher-level skills to analyze and interpret text, they can use this knowledge to successfully comprehend any text.

Reading Strategies	Reading Skills
• Predicting	• Retelling
• Making Connections	• Sequencing
• Visualizing	• Main Idea
• Clarifying	• Theme
• Questioning	• Cause/Effect
• Inferencing	• Character Traits
• Drawing Conclusions	• Compare/Contrast
• Summarizing	• Conflict/Resolution

Text selection is imperative when teaching strategies and skills. Remember, reading strategies can be taught using any book, any genre, or any grade level. Text should be strategically selected to match a particular reading skill. I love incorporating themes and content objectives when possible to teach particular strategies or skills. A few examples are provided below.

Book Title	Reading Skill	Theme/Content Standard
The Greedy Triangle	Character Traits	Math/Geometry/Shapes
If You Give a… series	Cause/Effect	Author/Series study
Cinderella stories	Compare/Contrast	Fairy tales/Diversity
Be You	Theme	One of a Kind
Wemberly Worried	Retelling	Overcoming Obstacles

Sample Student Work in Comprehension

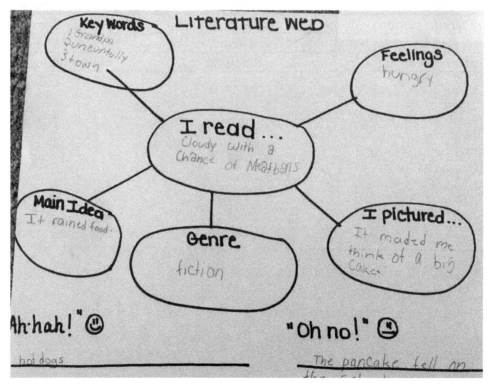

Using Mysteries to teach Comprehension Skills
Becoming a Reading Detective

Introduction:
1. Mystery Readers
2. Missing Person or Character
3. Solve a real mystery in school

> ➢ Making Predictions-predict what the mystery will be based on the book title and/or chapter titles
> ➢ Identify and describe the setting-understand and infer how multiple settings are present in one selection and why each are so important to solving the mystery
> ➢ "I wonder" questions should be used before, during, and after reading so the reader can use inference and prediction skills to solve the mystery
> ➢ Identify and describe the characters-when the reader understands that every character in a mystery is considered a suspect, they are more likely to remember details of the character throughout the text

Mystery Reader

Today, our mystery reader was _____.

We listened to the book, _____.

My favorite part of the book was _____

_____

_____.

Detective Case File

Reading Detective: _____

Book Title: _____

Characters:

Suspects	Witnesses

Settings:

Clues (in order)

How is the mystery solved? What evidence helped crack the case?

Mystery Series

- *The Boxcar Children* series by Gertrude Chandler Warner
- *The Babysitters Club* series by Ann M. Martin
- *Young Cam Jansen/Cam Jansen* by David Adler
- *Sugar Creek Gang Mystery Series* by Paul Hutchins
- *Backpack Mysteries* by Mary Carpenter Reid
- *Hardy Boys* series by Franklin W. Dixon
- *Nancy Drew* mysteries by Carolyn M. Keene
- *Encyclopedia Brown* series by Donald J. Sobel
- *Hank the Cowdog* series by John R. Erickson
- *Wishbone Mysteries* by Anne Capeci
- *Jigsaw Jones* Mystery series by James Preller
- *Carmen Sandiego* mysteries by Melissa Peterson
- *Nate the Great* series by Marjorie W. Sharmat
- *A to Z Mysteries* by Ron Roy

Let's Clarify!

Name _____

Use the chart below to organize your thoughts. Let's clarify what we are reading!

Title _____

Author _____

What the text says…	What the character thinks and/or does…	What it really means…

Teacher Tip: *Amelia Bedelia* books are ideal for this activity.

Minerva Louise at School

Objective: to clarify meaning when reading

What Minerva thought the object was...	What the object really was...
fancy barn	
farmer	
laundry	
stalls	
animals	
cow milking stools	
pig pen	
chicken feed bucket	
nesting boxes	
ribbon	
fur	
egg	
hay	

Story Words

Directions: Use picture clues and background knowledge to create a story word chart before reading. Write words, phrases, and ideas that you think will appear in reading.

Title:
Setting(s):
Theme:

Name _____

Book _____

Who?	Where?

What Happened?

My favorite setting is _____

because _____

_____

_____

_____

```
┌─────────────────────────────────────────┐
│                                           │
│                                           │
│                                           │
│                                           │
│                                           │
│                                           │
│                                           │
│                                           │
│                                           │
│                                           │
│                                           │
│                                           │
│                                           │
└─────────────────────────────────────────┘
```

Picture Title:

Name _____

Making a Mind Movie

A mind movie is how you visualize the text you are reading.

What is the title of the text, chapter, or chapter book you are reading?

_____

Beginning   **Middle**   **End**

_____   _____   _____

_____   _____   _____

_____   _____   _____

_____   _____   _____

Visualizing My Book

Title of Book _____

I see….	I hear…
I smell…	I taste…
I feel…	I imagine…

Book Summary Club

Name _____

Title of Story: _____

Author: _____

Directions: The code is SWBSTF (**S**omebody **W**anted **B**ut **S**o **T**hen **F**inally). Write a summary about the story by completing the following summary sentence. Then add detail in a picture below.

_____ wanted

_____

, but_____

_____, so

_____.

Then, _____

Finally, _____

_____.

126

Mother Goose Summaries

Name _____

Directions: A summary is a short overview of what happened in a poem or book. There is a code that must be followed. (SWBS-Somebody Wanted But So) Think about these popular Mother Goose rhymes and complete a summary for each one.

1. *Jack and Jill*

_____ wanted _____,

but _____,

so _____.

2. *Little Bo Peep*

_____ wanted _____,

but _____,

so _____.

3. *Little Miss Muffet*

_____ wanted _____,

but _____,

so _____.

4. *Humpty Dumpty*

_____ wanted _____,

but _____,

so _____.

Fairy tale/Folk tale Summaries

Name _____

Directions A summary is a short overview of what happened in a poem or book. There is a code that must be followed. (SWBS-Somebody Wanted But So) Think about these popular Mother Goose rhymes and complete a summary for each one.

1. *The Three Bears*

_____ wanted _____,

but _____,

so _____.

2. *The Three Little Pigs*

_____ wanted _____,

but _____,

so _____.

3. *The Little Red Hen*

_____ wanted _____,

but _____,

so _____.

4. *The Gingerbread Man*

_____ wanted _____,

but _____,

so _____.

Listening Comprehension

Title: _____

Author: _____

Illustrator: _____

WHO are the characters? _____

_____

WHERE does the story take place? _____

_____

WHEN does the story take place? _____

_____

WHAT happened? _____

_____

_____

_____

Did you like this story? _____ WHY or WHY not?

_____

_____

Summary vs. Retelling
(in student language)

Retelling: <u>Tell</u> all of the details of the story from beginning to end like the person you're telling it to has never read the story.

Summary: Giving <u>some</u> of the key facts or details of the story. Provide the overall theme or gist of the text.

Lesson: Summarizing Nonfiction Passages
1. Students read a one to two paragraph nonfiction passion.
2. Students create a title for the passage related to the main idea. Teachers write a list of the suggested titles and see how many are similar, thus closely representing the main idea of the passage.
3. Students highlight or underline key facts or ideas in the passage.
4. Students write a one to two sentence news reporter synopsis to summarize the passage. (Students should imagine they are a news reporter and only have 30 seconds to report the story. This forces them to pick out the most important pieces to relay the information to the listener or reader.)

Sequencing

Activity 1: Use a pocket chart and sentence strips to put poems and sentences from selected stories in order.

Activity 2: Read any version of *The Gingerbread Man*. Complete the sentences below to match your version. Students will cut out the sentence strips and put them in the correct order to match the retelling of the story.

The gingerbread _____ is chased by the _____
The gingerbread _____ is chased by the _____
The family decided to make gingerbread cookies.
The gingerbread _____ says "You can't catch me!" and runs away.
The gingerbread _____ hops off the cookie sheet.

Main Idea Menu

Welcome to the Main Idea Restaurant where we only serve the <u>Most Important</u> dishes. Our food is prepared with the <u>Big Picture</u> in mind.

I. **Appetizers: just a title of the book or poem-** Based on the titles below, what do you think the main idea of the story will be?

    a. *Just Shopping with Mom*

    _____

    b. *The Greedy Triangle*

    _____

    c. *So You Want to be President*

    _____

    d. *The Treehouse Adventure*

    _____

II. **Entrée: the main course-** Listen to this chapter of a book. Think about the big idea, not the dirty details. Use that main idea to predict the title of the book or chapter.

_____

III. **Dessert: the creative masterpiece-** On the back, draw a picture to illustrate one of the main ideas below.

    a. The Lesson   b. Growing Pains   c. The Washout

Themes Presented in Fairy Tales

Name: _____

A **theme** is the message of a story. We may learn something new about ourselves or remind us of important phrases, values, or life lessons we experience every day. Books and movies always have a theme. Read and think about the themes below. Use the word bank of fairy tale titles to match the correct title to its theme.

Sleeping Beauty	Beauty and the Beast	The Elves and the Shoemaker
The Emperor's New Clothes	Cinderella	The Frog Prince

1. "Don't judge a book by its cover."

2. "True love conquers all."

3. "Too much pride or vanity is not something you want to have."

4. "Hard work pays off in the end."

5. "Chase your dream."

6. "It is important to treat everyone fairly."

Main Idea Match-up

Name _____

Look at the photo of the day. Make up a story title for each one.

A. _____

B. _____

C. _____

D. _____

E. _____

Match the main idea with its best detail.

1. We had a fun day at the beach. _____

2. The football game was close. _____

3. Our trip to the farm was an adventure. _____

4. The garden was growing so quickly. _____

5. Which one is your classroom? _____

A. The pigs and chickens were running around.

B. It has about twenty desks.

C. The sand felt good on my toes.

D. Both teams made touchdowns.

E. The pretty tulips were in full bloom.

The MVP (Most Valuable Part)

The VIP (Very Important Part)

Identifying, understanding, and explaining the main idea in a nonfiction text can be a challenging task for teachers and students. Consider adding the following ideas.

- ➤ **Use the title to tell a possible story**
- ➤ **Draw a main idea table (main idea and four supporting details)**
- ➤ **Ask students to read text to create the headings and titles (more often than not, they choose the main idea)**
- ➤ **Write a one sentence summary**
- ➤ **Paragraph Pencil Sketch: Students will draw a pencil sketch beside each paragraph. More often than not, they draw the most important part, which is needed to determine the main idea. Once each paragraph has a pencil sketch, students should determine the main idea of the text. This practice can also be used to summarize a text in one two three sentences.**

It Happens!!!

Name _____

*Use your background knowledge to decide either what caused each event below to happen or what happened because of something.

CAUSE	EFFECT
	The seats in the car were soaking wet when I got in the back seat that morning.
	I got up late and had to get a tardy slip when I got to school.
I was playing basketball inside the house.	
	The electricity went out in our house last night.
I studied my multiplication facts every night before the quiz.	

What caused this to happen?   **This is the effect!**

138

Our School has Facts and Opinions

Name _____

A <u>fact</u> is a statement that can be proven true.
An <u>opinion</u> is one person's idea or feeling.

Directions: Read each sentence below. Decide if each statement is a fact or an opinion. Write F beside it for fact. Write O beside it for an opinion.

1. There are twenty students in our reading class. _
2. The gym is bigger than the classroom.
3. Math is my favorite subject. __
4. *Green Eggs and Ham* is the most popular book by Dr. Seuss.
5. The school is located on Maplewood Avenue.
6. She is the coolest teacher.
7. We have a male assistant principal.
8. There are more fifth grade teachers than second grade teachers in our school.
9. I can't wait for third grade!
10. He is the best PE teacher ever!

*Make up two sentences about your school. Have your neighbor guess which sentence is a fact and which one is an opinion.

Recipe: How to Make Mooncakes
*From frankasch.com/recipes/

Ingredients:
3 eggs
Dash of salt
¼ cup of Grape Nuts
Dash of cinnamon
Butter
Maple Syrup (preferably real Vermont maple syrup)

Procedure:
1. Melt a small amount of butter into an omelette pan.
2. Beat eggs lightly, add dash of salt, and pour into pan.
3. Let cook on medium to low flame for about 30 seconds.
4. Sprinkle grape nuts on top of eggs.
5. Add cinnamon and let it cook until bottom is light brown.
6. Flip carefully and let the other side cook until done.
7. Serve with butter and maple syrup as you would a pancake.
**Bear prefers his with honey. Mmm delicious!!

Using the recipe, answer the following questions.
1. A fraction is needed of what ingredient? _____
2. What two ingredients require the same amount?

_____   _____
3. Where should the maple syrup really be from? _____
4. What is a synonym for *beat*? _____
5. Do you cook on medium for more or less than a minute? _____
6. What is a word in the procedure that rhymes with *clip*? _____
7. What food do we eat that is most similar to a mooncake? _____
8. What would Bear use honey in place of in this recipe? _____
9. Which of the following action steps comes after you cook? Flip, add, or melt? _____
10. What would happen if you did not flip the mooncake?

_____

Literacy across the Content All Year Long

Teaching with Trade Books

Title of Book	Unit of Study	Reading Level
Red, White, and Blue	Patriotism	K
Grow Flower Grow	Plant Life Cycle	1
It's Pumpkin Time	Plant Life Cycle	1 (late)
Red Eyed Tree Frog	Habitats/Animals	1 (late)
Are you my Mother?	Animals	1 (late)
Officer Buckle and Gloria	Citizenship	2
Me on the Map	Map Skills	2
The Very Hungry Caterpillar	Butterfly Life Cycle	2
My Teacher for President	Patriotism	2
Duck for President	Patriotism	2
The Mixed-Up Chameleon	Adaptations	2
Frog and Toad Books	Frog Life Cycle	2
Froggy Books	Frog Life Cycle	2
The Ox-Cart Man	Economics	2
The Chipmunk at Hollow Tree Lane	Hibernation	2
Bill and Pete Go Down the Nile	Egypt	2
Go to Sleep Groundhog	Hibernation	2
Martin's Big Words	Famous Americans	2
Happy Birthday Moon	Earth Cycles	2
The Grouchy Ladybug	Time	2 (late)
A Picture Book of Rosa Parks	Famous Americans	2 (late)
Cloudy with a Chance of Meatballs	Weather	2 (late)
Stellaluna	Animals	3
The Lorax	Economics	3
Turtle Without a Home	Ecosystems	3
Amy's Travels	Continents	3
Chester the Worldly Pig	Continents	3
Magic School Bus Inside the Earth	Earth	3
George Washington's Breakfast	Famous Americans	3 (late)
The Greedy Triangle	Geometry	3 (late)
The Great Kapok Tree	Habitats	4
Just a Dream	Environment	4
The Watsons Go to Birmingham	Civil Rights	5

Putting the Pieces Together

How many experiences a day are we providing for our students in reading, writing, and word work? When we effectively implement the five pillars of reading into any small or whole group lesson (including science or social studies), we are providing the best instruction to help students become successful readers. We should also strategically plan using paired text that match a theme, reading standard, or content objective. Consider how to add writing and literacy extensions to support your lesson throughout the week. When students are independently working during guided reading time, they should be given assignments that are review and be completed without teacher assistance. Disruptive behaviors most often occur when a task is too hard to complete. When we think about how some students may be working on their own for at least thirty minutes, we need to plan valuable experiences instead of "busy work." How do we put it all together?

Lesson Example 1: *The Paperboy* **by Dav Pilkey**

Theme/Topic: Responsibility or Author Study

Background Knowledge: Does your family get the newspaper delivered? Bring in multiple copies of your local newspaper for students to touch and read over.

Phonological Awareness (oral): Compound words
Teacher says: "Newspaper" is a compound word. Two words are put together to make a new word. When we a cut the word in half-news and paper are the two words. Paperboy is also a compound word. What two words make the compound word paperboy?

Vocabulary: Introduce *route, fade, gazette* prior to reading using a suggested vocabulary activity from the book

Comprehension: How does setting impact the story? (Story Elements)
Graphic Organizer-

Where?	When?	What happened?

Phonics: Select words from the text to support grade level or instructional reading level phonics standards. In this text, focus on the CVCe pattern (fade, race, home, time, bike, ride). Ask students to explain how these words are alike? Sort the words by long vowel sound.

Fluency: If this is a small group lesson, fluency takes place when the students whisper or silently reads at their own pace while the teacher listens in. If this is a whole group lesson, scaffold the instruction appropriately by grade level. Read the grade level text to the students, encourage students to read in pairs, and support students reading on their own. Choose particular phrases to chorally read together. Never chorally read the entire text.

Writing: What is the young boy dreaming about? When are you the happiest?

Extensions: Use newspapers to complete a word hunt for CVCe words or to review text features.

Lesson Example 1: *Amy's Travels* **by Kathryn Starke**

Theme/Topic: Seven Continents (social studies)

Background Knowledge: Use a world map and globe to show students where the seven continents on earth are located in relation to their home city, state, and country. Take a virtual field trip to each continent. Complete the sorting activity on the following page.

Phonological Awareness (oral): ask students to tell you how many syllables are in each of the seven continent names when you say them aloud

Vocabulary: continent, safari, experienced

Comprehension: Compare/contrast (continents, school, animal life, etc.)

Phonics: -tion; vacation, transportation, location

Fluency: If this is a small group lesson, fluency takes place when the students whisper or silently reads at their own pace while the teacher listens in. If this is a whole group lesson, scaffold the instruction appropriately by grade level. Read the grade level text to the students, encourage students to read in pairs, and support students reading on their own. Choose particular phrases to chorally read together. Never chorally read the entire text.

Writing: What continent will you visit first?

Extensions: Research of a specific city or landmark around the world. Create a travel brochure, tourism commercial, or write and illustrate a postcard from the location.

Directions: Sort the following cities, landmarks, or features under the correct continent.

Antarctica	North America	Australia
South America	Europe	Asia
Africa	United States	Statue of Liberty
Safari	penguins	kangaroos
Great Wall of China	Eiffel Tower	Washington DC
Brazil	Italy	ice
Queen of England	koala bears	Japan

Sample Book Guide

Title of Book _____**Grade** _____
Unit of Study _____

Questioning:
Before Reading:

During Reading:

After Reading:

Classroom Extensions/Other Resources:

It's Measurement Time!
by Kathryn Starke

What do you want to measure?
There are so many options to choose,
Distance or weather, objects, or liquid,
Food, or even you!

How do we measure these items?
A ruler, a yard stick, a scale?
These tools are all very useful.
We have to pick one that works well.

As soon as you've measured your treasure,
Make sure it makes perfect sense!
Would you ever measure an elephant and say,
"Oh, it's just five ounces…. I think."

Take time to make guesses
Then measure away,
You'll be dreaming in "meters"
Day after day!

The Atoms Family

(Tune of *The Addams Family*)
by Kathryn Starke

They're tiny parts of matter
Can't seem them from a ladder
And often times they scatter
The Atoms Family!

Matter has three phases
Solids, liquids, gases
You measure it by masses
The Atoms Family!

One change is chemical
One change is physical
Ice is a solid, water's a liquid, vapor's a gas.

So, check around for objects
They're taking space around us
Yes, matter does surround us,
The Atoms Family!

Month by Month Planning
Back to School Season

We all have amnesia in the new school year. We said goodbye to a group of students almost three months prior after watching them becoming mature, independent young readers and writers. We have created a new classroom theme and are excited about our new class. Then, after a few weeks of instruction we administer a literacy assessment and are so upset with the results. We are convinced this is the "lowest class" we have ever had. I am going to stop you right there. You already forgot about last year's class makeup and everything you did as an instructional leader to help your students become so successful. Now is the time when you determine your mindset, which should be the following. My students determine my instruction. because they let me know their strengths and challenges.

Do not wait until reading assessments are given to begin small group and one-on-one reading instruction. Yes, there was a slide. Yes, the students are starting the year "below benchmark." When you create an environment that promotes literacy from the first day of school, you will help your students thrive as readers and writers before the assessment is given. Use the diagnostic tools listed later in this book to better plan your reading instruction.

Back to School Lessons

- ➢ ABC Scavenger Hunt Around the Room
- ➢ Descriptive Name or Interest Acrostic Poem

    Example: **K**ind   **K**angaroos

             Active   **A**riana Grande

             Talkative   **T**ravel

- ➢ Bulletin Board: My first day I felt _____because_____. (photos of children)
- ➢ Sticker Partner Interview: Distribute pairs of stickers around the classroom for students to find their matching sticker and interview each other. Encourage children to ask questions to their partner to learn more about their last school year, summer, and favorite things.
- ➢ Back to School Books
- ➢ Back to School Bulletin Boards Highlighting Student Names:
  - A Glance into 2nd Grade (windowpanes)
  - Cruise into a New year (ships or cars)
  - A Bubbly New Class (bubbles)
  - Here is the Scoop: 1st grade is a real treat (ice cream)
  - Second Graders Hard at Work (construction site)
- ➢ Label your classroom with object names and phrases including scientists, authors, explorers, readers, and mathematicians.

Name _____

Directions: Complete the sentence below and draw a picture to match.

When I grow up, I want to be a _____
because _____.

Suggested Fall Semester Ideas

- ➢ September 13th-author Roald Dahl's birthday; author study in this book
- ➢ September 22nd-Post Office established; letter writing lesson
- ➢ September 26th-Johnny Appleseed's birthday; apple adjectives and recipes
- ➢ September Bulletin Board: Falling into Great Work
- ➢ October-National Pizza Month; descriptive paragraph about pizza
- ➢ October 31st-Halloween; write a candy wrapper story based on candy treats
- ➢ October Bulletin Board: All Caught up in Good Work (spider web)
- ➢ November-Election Day; voting on books
- ➢ November-Thanksgiving; turkey feather rhymes
- ➢ November Bulletin Board: Welcome to our Banquet of Knowledge
- ➢ December-Holidays around the World

Planning Ahead

When you use daily holidays or pop culture to teach reading and writing, students are engaged in learning. When I was a first grader, I remember we had a "teddy bear day". We all brought in our favorite stuffed teddy bear and went to the cafeteria for a morning snack of biscuits and honey. When I was a third grader, we had "pig day". My mom put my hair in pigtails, we spoke pig Latin in school, and all of our reading and writing activities were related to pigs. The rest of this chapter provides holiday themed poems, lessons, reading contracts, and end of year activities that I hope will provide a memorable teaching and learning experience for you and your students.

Visualizing Thanksgiving

Directions: Read the sentences below to answer the questions. Visualize exactly what the words are saying.

1. Which sentence helps you visualize what the turkey looked like?
    a. The turkey tasted delicious.
    b. The turkey felt soft and smooth.
    c. The turkey was big, brown, and juicy on the outside.
    d. The turkey took forever to prepare.

2. Which sentence allows you to visualize the pumpkin pie?
    a. I want more pumpkin pie!
    b. The pumpkin pie reminds me of Thanksgiving.
    c. I predict the pumpkin pie will taste great.
    d. The sweet-smelling pumpkin pie had whipped cream on top.

3. Which sentence below helps you visualize Thanksgiving at home?
    a. We watched the parade.
    b. Our family gathered around the table for a feast of food.
    c. We ate turkey.
    d. The mashed potatoes were excellent.

4. Which sentence makes you visualize the first Thanksgiving?
    a. The Pilgrims and Native Americans were there.
    b. The Pilgrims and Native Americans had a feast.
    c. The Pilgrims and Native Americans gathered around the table together to enjoy an amazing feast.
    d. The Native Americans hunted animals for the feast.

Gingerbread Men Fingerplay and Chant
(Adapted by Kathryn Starke)

Five little gingerbread men lying on a tray,
One jumped up and ran away.
Shouting, "Catch me, catch me, catch me if you can…
I run really fast, I'm a gingerbread man!"

Four little gingerbread men lying on a tray,
One jumped up and ran away.
Shouting, "Catch me, catch me, catch me if you can…
I run really fast, I'm a gingerbread man!"

Three little gingerbread men lying on a tray,
One jumped up and ran away.
Shouting, "Catch me, catch me, catch me if you can…
I run really fast, I'm a gingerbread man!"

Two little gingerbread men lying on a tray,
One jumped up and ran away.
Shouting, "Catch me, catch me, catch me if you can…
I run really fast, I'm a gingerbread man!"

One little gingerbread man lying on a tray,
One jumped up and ran away.
Shouting, "Catch me, catch me, catch me if you can…
I run really fast, I'm a gingerbread man!"

No more gingerbread men lying on a tray,
They all jumped up and ran away.
Oh, how I wish they had stayed with me to play.
Next time I'll eat them before they run away.

Five Little Presents
(Adapted and created by Kathryn Starke)

Five little presents sitting on the floor,
One said, "It's time for me to head out the door."

Four little presents sitting on a log,
One said, "How can we travel with all of this fog?"

Three little sisters sitting on a rug,
One said, "I could really use a hug."

Two little presents sitting on the stair,
One said, "Doesn't anyone care?"

One little present sitting on a gate,
It said, "I hope the holidays don't come late!"

JANUARY READING CONTRACT

Name_____

Books I Read This Month:

_____

Check off each activity that you complete below.

_____ Using the title and cover picture only, make a prediction of what your story will be about. You must tell someone before you read so that at the end of the book, you can ask them ii your prediction was correct. Talk about the book together.

_____ Write a note to someone in your family telling them about the chapter or book you are reading this week. Clarify for them the characters, setting, and problem.

_____ Tell an adult the connections you are making while you read-a connection to yourself, to another text, and to the world.

_____ Draw a picture to show a visualization of what you are reading. Imagine the book is a movie. What do you see?

_____ Write 5 questions that you would ask the main character in an interview.

_____ You have finished the book. Pretend you are the author of the next chapter or next book. What will happen next?

_____ Go on a word hunt. Write down any word you see that matches your word study pattern this week.

_____ Write a letter to your teacher about your favorite part of the book you read and why. She needs lots of detail. If it is great, she will write back to you!

FEBRUARY READING CONTRACT

Name._____

Books I Read This Month:

_____
_____
_____
_____

Check off each activity that you complete below.

_____ Describe the setting, characters, and most important event in our story. Write at least one sentence for each story element.

_____ Abraham Lincoln loved to read. Write him a letter recommending a book you have recently read. Tell him what makes it so enjoyable to read.

_____ Tell an adult the connections you are making while you read-a connection to yourself, to another text, and to the world.

_____ Make a valentine for the main character in your book. Describe the character's traits (positive and negative).

_____ What is the author's purpose for writing this book?

_____ Go on a word hunt: write down any word you see that matches your word study pattern this week.

_____ Pretend you write an advice column for a magazine, newspaper, or blog. You need to identify the problem in the story and give advice as to how to solve that particular problem.

_____ Write a love letter to your favorite character or author.

Valentine's Day Poems

Five little valentines were having a race.
The first little valentine was frilly with lace.
The second little valentine had a funny face.
The third little valentine said, "I love you."
The fourth little valentine said, "I do too."
The fifth little valentine was as sly as a fox.
He ran the fastest to the valentine box.

Five little valentines just for you.
The first one says, "My love is true."
The second one says, "You have my heart."
The third one says, "Let us never part."
The fourth one says, "Won't you please be mine?"
The fifth one says, "'Til the end of time."

March Reading Contract

Name _____

Books I Read This Month:

_____

_____

*Check off each activity that you complete below.

_____Describe the setting, characters, and most important events in your story. Write at least one sentence for each story element.

_____You are going to school disguised as one of the characters in the book. Who will you choose? What will you look like? How will you act in school that day?

_____Tell an adult the connection you are making while you read-a connection to yourself, to another text, and to the world.

_____Imagine this story took place in the past. How would the characters, setting, and events be different? Explain.

_____Write a new ending for the story. You may change anything you want!

_____Go on a word hunt. Write down any word you see that matches your word study pattern this week.

_____Pretend you have the power to bring good luck to any character in the book. How would you help?

Five Little Leprechauns
(Adapted and Created by Kathryn Starke)

Five little leprechauns dancing in the woods,
The first one said, "I wish I could!"
The second one said, "I can try!"
The third one said, "Oh me, oh my!"
The fourth one said, "I'm way too slow."
The fifth one said, "Here we go!"
He snapped his fingers 1,2,3
And made a pot of gold for all to see!

Directions: Write a letter to a future _____ grader who may be in this class next year.

Date _____

Dear _____,

Sincerely,

_____

Summary Reading Calendar

Week 1

Monday	Tuesday	Wednesday	Thursday	Friday
Check out books about female founders, scientists, or philanthropists that are interesting to you. Write a letter to her telling her asking for advice.	What is your favorite holiday? Write about it and find a book that uses your favorite holiday as the setting.	Let's learn about our family heritage, culture, and traditions. Interview family members and take a virtual visit to the countries of origin that match your family's background.	You can now Tackle Reading at home month with NFL/NFLA athletes sharing their favorite books. Check out football themed titles when you search #TackleReading.	Summer is upon us. Go outside and make an observation of the seasonal weather. Read books about summer, the beach, pool, or summer sports.

Week 2

Monday	Tuesday	Wednesday	Thursday	Friday
Watch a forecast today from a local meteorologist. Check out books on rain, weather, storms, and precipitation. Finish this prompt with something fun to illustrate like "cats and dogs." "It's raining_____."	Take a walk around your neighborhood in search of flower or vegetable gardens. Read books about plants, gardens, and flowers.	If you could start your own business, what product or service would you offer? Check out the children's book series "Mr. Business" by BK Fulton today for some fun stories and helpful tips.	While sports are on hold, I want you to think about some titles you would put in your book brackets. Read some basketball, baseball, or sports themed titles.	What are your goals and dreams? Write them all down today. Read *Kickin' It with Kenzie* written by a third grader. She shares her ideas on what's meant to be.

Week 3

Monday	Tuesday	Wednesday	Thursday	Friday
While we cannot always travel overseas, we can visit Paris and London in the Two Mice travel series by Donna Dalton. If you could travel anywhere today, where would you go? Why?	Pack a picnic of anything you want for lunch today with your family. Write a descriptive paragraph about what foods, drinks, and treats you would include.	Have you ever read Anansi's trickster tales or know a trickster in your life or in another book to read today?	What is your favorite children's book? Choose any book you would like to read today and write a book review about it.	Take a trip around the world in less than 20 minutes by reading *Amy's Travels* by Kathryn Starke. After reading, write your response to Amy's question. What continent would you visit first?

Week 4

Monday	Tuesday	Wednesday	Thursday	Friday
What is a gladiator? Read *The Little Gladiator* by Joel Gamble to see how this NFL alumni athlete author portrays a gladiator.	Read books about pets and take a virtual (or live if available) trip to a local park or nature center with these adorable animals.	Have you ever heard of the story *Jellybeans for Breakfast*? Can you imagine?	Read nonfiction books about animals that either hatch from or lay eggs. Become an expert and write the top five facts you learned.	Read funny, serious, and seasonal poetry. Write your own poem. Share them at a family tea party.

Week 5

Monday	Tuesday	Wednesday	Thursday	Friday
Take a virtual trip to the zoo. Read books about zoo animals. Create a map of your own zoo labeling all of your favorite animals. Bonus points if you include a map key.	Let's read books about music, sing, play instruments, and have a dance party. If someone in your family plays guitar, I am most impressed.	What do you dream about doing when you get older? Write down your goals to make them come true.	Go online to your local library to reserve some books to check out or make a list of 3 books or topics you want to check out when you return to the library.	Have you ever gone cloud watching? Go outside, sit on the grass, and look up. What do you see in the clouds? Draw a picture or write a story.

Week 6

Monday	Tuesday	Wednesday	Thursday	Friday
Host a popcorn party! What is your favorite book that has been turned into a movie? Compare and contrast the book and movie.	Give somebody a hug or high five today! Read books about love, hugs, and friendship.	Read books about earth, recycling, and conservation. Take a walk around your neighborhood enjoying our earth.	How can you work with a family member today at home or in their office? Write a detailed job description.	So many people have had birthdays this spring and have not been able to celebrate with a party. Create an invitation and plan the perfect party for yourself to celebrate you.

Week 7

Monday	Tuesday	Wednesday	Thursday	Friday
What is your favorite food? Find your favorite recipe and make it today.	Let's host a teddy bear picnic. Grab your favorite teddy bear, blanket, and pack a snack to eat together outside.	Have you ever camped in a tent under the moon or stars in your backyard? Take a flashlight and your favorite camping stories.	Send a letter or postcard to someone in the mail that you wish you could see this summer.	Host an ice cream sundae party for your family. Make a list of your family's favorite ice cream flavors.

Week 8

Monday	Tuesday	Wednesday	Thursday	Friday
Who doesn't love bubbles? You can make bubbles in a big dish or find some at the store and enjoy them outside.	Draw a picture of fireworks and write five words that describe them. Did you see any this summer?	What is the tallest building you have ever seen? Have you ever seen a skyscraper? Let's find books about towers and build one today.	Read some nonfiction books about sharks and write down five fascinating facts that you learned about them.	Have you ever been on a train? Where would you go? Read books about trains and transportation today.

Week 9

Monday	Tuesday	Wednesday	Thursday	Friday
How are you feeling today? Write about it and draw the color that matches your mood.	Celebrate hat day! Wear your favorite hat all day long today. How do you feel when you wear it?	What is your favorite board game to play? Set up a game table today for your family. Read the directions carefully.	Enjoy a beach day. Put on your sunglasses and read outside some books about the beach or summer vacation.	What is your favorite Disney character or movie? Look for a folk tale or fairy tale that a movie or character was based on.

Week 10

Monday	Tuesday	Wednesday	Thursday	Friday
Community helpers are essential workers. Who are they in your community? Read books and articles about their work.	Comics have appeared in the newspaper for decades. Find a comic book or comic strip today that makes you laugh out loud.	An inventor brings an idea to life. Read about a famous invention or inventor in our world.	What is your favorite hobby? Have you ever read books about someone who has turned your hobby into a business?	Read a book about a favorite artist then color, draw, paint, or create something special to highlight your summer.

Writing

Writing in the classroom is just as important as reading, and unfortunately, it is often cut from the school day. We should be encouraging writers as well as readers. When children see how reading and writing are strongly connected through words, their literacy knowledge greatly increases. More often than not, a child's reading level is higher than their writing level because they are given more opportunities to decode rather than encode each day. Select a writing sample from one of your students. What is the child's reading level? Does their reading level match their writing level? What word knowledge do they have in reading that they are not using in their writing? When we hold our students accountable to incorporate their reading and word knowledge in their writing, we see better results in all three areas of literacy.

Does your classroom support young authors? In addition to writing lessons, my students had writing partners from another classroom and pen pals from another school. In order to spark ideas and promote creativity, I implemented time writing biweekly. Every morning, my students wrote in a journal to a prompt unless it was "free choice Friday." My students also looked forward to the opportunity to taking our class stuffed animal home on weekend and recording their journey together. The student shared the adventure every Monday morning by reading aloud their own writing. In the primary grades, I put together homemade class books written by the students. These were part of the reading corner for students to read during independent reading time. In the spring, turned my classroom into a publishing company. The students pitched me their story or article idea then worked at their own pace on the writing, editing, and illustrating before publishing their original work. We celebrated with a publishing party and displayed their books in the school library.

This chapter provides activities and lessons that support writing instruction. The following list outlines all of the aspects of writing that should be taught in the elementary school classroom.

- Mini Lessons: Components and Conventions in Writing (Writing Traits and Grammar)
- The Writing Process (sequence)
- Creative Writing/Choice Writing
- Writing to a Prompt/Dice Writing
- Writing Across the Content
- Writing About Reading
- Writing Genres

Homemade Class Books

Steps:
1. Select an appropriate topic, theme, or sentence starter for K-2 students.
2. Provide a piece of paper for each student to write and draw their page.
3. Collect the pages and put together in a classroom book for reading time.

Sample Ideas:
- My favorite season is _____ because _____.
- My favorite color is _____ because _____.
- When I grow up, I want to be a _____ because _____.
- My favorite breakfast food is _____.
- My favorite sport is _____.
- If I were the President of the United States, I would…
- If I were the teacher, I would…
- If I could start any business, I would…
- If I lived in a snowglobe…
- On the weekends, I love to _____.
- My favorite book is _____ because _____.
- If I could visit anywhere in the world, I would go to _____.
- My favorite animal is _____ because _____.
- My Family
- A Trip to the Zoo
- My Summer Vacation
- A Trip to Space

Timed Writing: Grades 3 and up

Steps:
1. Students should have a piece of paper and pencil ready to go.
2. The teacher will read aloud a story starter for students to listen carefully to and determine how many minutes the students will write the entire time for today. Start with five minutes and work up to twenty minutes adding two to three minutes over a period of time.
3. When the teacher says *start*, the students write as much as they can. Spelling, grammar, punctuation does not count. This exercise is all about creativity and formulating ideas.
4. When the teacher says *stop,* the students will put their pencils down and count up the amount of words they wrote. Several weeks of writing using the same of number of minutes will allow for comparison of amount of words written.

Sample Story Starters:
- One sunny day, I was wandering around the neighborhood and saw bubbles in the air coming from one yard. I followed the bubbles as far as I could until I was flying in a bubble myself.
- We were working on our laptops when lightning suddenly hit our school, and the power went out. The classroom became dark, quiet, and strange. When the lights finally came back on, our teacher was gone and standing in the front of the room was…
- We went on a trip to a ranch to learn how to ride and take care of horses. I learned how to brush and feed the horse. One afternoon, I put on my riding boots and hopped up on the saddle to ride. I decided to ride as fast as I could until…

Let's Make it a Complete Thought!

Name _____

Directions: Find out if the **Who?** Or **What?** is missing and fill in the blank.

1. _____chased after the cat.

2. _____gave lots of homework.

3. The baby _____.

4. He _____.

5. The car _____.

6. The girl _____.

OUR ROYAL PUNCTUATION FAMILY

__Prince Period__-Duty: to end a telling sentence
__Queen Question Mark__-Duty: to ask a question
__Count of Comma__-Duty: to combine two sentences, separate items in a series,
to separate the city from a state, the date, or the greeting of a letter

Directions: Read each sentence below and add the correct punctuation.

1. Do you know what time it is

2. I prefer pineapple on my pizza

3. I was born in Richmond Virginia

4. Where is the nurse

5. Travel should resume on January 2 2022

6. We like to shop and we like to go to the movies

7. I need to get apples oranges and grapes at the store

8. When will the mail arrive

**Now, it's your turn! Write 3 sentences for your classmates to read and add the correct punctuation.

Scrambled Sentences

Directions: Cut up sentence boxes below and put in alphabetical order to create a complete sentence.

to	babies	wiggle	like

home	come	now

time	he	is	on

avocado	are	almonds	and	yummy

am	punctual	late	or	I

Name _____

Below are some letters I received from Obedience School. Unfortunately, Ike did not have a fourth-grade teacher to help him learn proper grammar. Please help me decipher the letters below.

Dear Mrs. LaRue,
How could you do this to me. This is a PRISON, not a scool! U should see the other dogs They are BAD DOGS, Mrs. LaRue! I do not fit in. even the journey hear was a horror. I am very unhappy and may need some thing to chew on when I get home Please come right away!
Sincerely
Ike

Dear mrs. LaRue
I hate to tell you this, but i am terribly ill. it started in my paw, causing me to limp all date. Later I felt queasy, so that I could bearly eat dinner (except for the yummy gravy). Then i began to moan and howl. Finally I had to be taken to the vet. Dr. Wilfrey claims that he can't find nothing wrong with me, but I am certain i have a awful disease. i must come home at once.
Honestly yours,
ike

Dear Mrs. laRue,
I continew to suffer horrible as I rome this barren wasteland. who knows where my wanderings will take me now. Hopefully to someplace with yummy food. remember the special treats you use to make for me? I miss them. I miss our nice comfy apartment But mostly, I miss you!
Your said dog,
Ike

P.S. I even miss the Hibbins' cats, in a way.

Now, check your editing skills by looking back at the book *Dear Mrs. LaRue!*

NOUNTOWN
(to the tune of "Downtown")
Created by Kathryn Starke

If you're a person or a place or a thing-
Then you will always be in Nountown.
Think of the people and the places you know,
Things all around will grow in Nountown.

Just think of all the people and the places that you know
Things around you just might begin to overflow.
How can you lose? The nouns are much brighter there
You can forget all your verbs and forgot all your cares
And go to Nountown!

People are great when you're in Nountown,
Places are for sure in Nountown,
Things will be waiting for you!

(Nountown-Nountown-Nountown)

Extension: Go on a noun scavenger hunt around the classroom or school. Give clues for students to guess the noun.
 Example: this noun has four legs on the ground

NOUN TALK

Name _____

    Last Friday after school, _____
                                           (person)

went to _____.He/she was so
                  (place)

excited when he/she spotted a _____.
                                  (thing)

The _____started to talk. Nobody
        (thing)

could understand what it was saying! Where are
we _____ shouted and the _____
      (person)   (thing)

responded _____.
              (place)

    This was no ordinary place! _____
                              (person)

looked up and down and left and right and
nothing looked familiar. The _____
                                    (thing)

started to get dark and _____decided it
                       (person)

was time to go home. He/she used a _____
                                (thing)

so he/she would be going in the right direction

to _____. Just as he/she could
         (place)

see _____, a _____
        (place)   (thing)

screamed out good-bye._____ ran to
                           (person)

_____ fast as he/she could
(place)

and did not look back once! What a day! ☺

Bump the Noun

Objective: to teach pronouns and how to use them in a sentence in place of nouns

Directions:
1. Distribute cards of pronouns to various students.
   (he, she, it, we, us, they, them, him, her)
2. Call on two students at a time to come to the front of the room holding a sentence. One should hold the subject and the other should hold the predicate.
3. The class chorally reads the sentence together.
4. Direct student in the class holding the correct subject pronoun to come to the front of the room and replace the noun. (Or the predicate pronoun-use teacher discretion)
5. The student will come to the front and "bump the noun." That student then sits down.
6. The class chorally reads the new sentence together.
7. Discuss why that pronoun is correct.

Example:
  Sarah and I are going to ride the bus to school tomorrow.
  We=correct pronoun to bump the subject/noun
  We are going to ride the bus to school tomorrow.
  Question: Who is the **we** in the sentence? Sarah and I

he	she	it
him	her	we
they	them	us

Sarah and I

are going to ride the bus to school tomorrow.

The boy

ran quickly to get to third base.

The teacher

spotted the three children hiding in the corner.

We

found the paintings hanging on the wall.

Eli and Malcolm

invited us to their house for the weekend.

Bump the Noun!

Name _____

Directions: Use the pronoun below to help you decide which nouns need to be replaced with the correct pronoun in the sentences below.

she	it	he	we	they

1. <u>Michael</u> was the first one to turn in his homework today.

    _____ was the first one to turn in his homework today.

2. <u>Melissa and I</u> had dinner at a new place.

    _____ had dinner at a new place.

3. <u>The book</u> was better than the movie!

    _____ was better than the movie!

4. <u>Jennifer</u> won first place in the science fair.

    _____ won first place in the science fair.

5. <u>Matt and Andrew</u> played ball all day Saturday.

    _____ played ball all day Saturday.

Chart Writing: Write a super sentence

Interactive Writing with students:
- Provide students with a picture, prompt, or theme to write about
- Example: If I were a scarecrow, Thanksgiving, or making money
- Based on your topic, the children will help you create a chart
- Include vivid verbs and amazing adjectives

Who or What?	Action Word (Did what?)	Where?	When?	Describing Word

- Complete each column one at a time

Example: If I were a scarecrow...

| scarecrow | run
play
scare
eat
fall
dance
sing
hide | cornfield
Richmond
farm
pumpkin
  patch
store | Thanksgiving
In the middle
  of the night
6AM
Last Monday | tiny
old
messy
nice
smart
wise
loud
quiet
tall |

- Then, have children write a super sentence by using one word from each column. It can be any order as long as it makes sense. They can add extra words (sight words) to have it make sense. Every child must have the word **scarecrow** as the *who* or *what* because that is the topic.

Example: The quiet scarecrow likes to hide in the cornfield in the middle of the night.

Example: I played with the nice scarecrow last Monday on the farm.

Example: Do you want to run and hide in the cornfield with the scarecrow this Thanksgiving Day?

Dice Writing

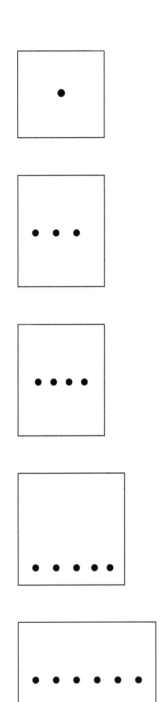

Assessing Growth and Reading Success: Home/School Connection

Reading Reflection at Home
*presented by Kathryn Starke

*The following questions can be used with any story to increase oral language skills and comprehension!

1. What do you think this story will be about? Use your picture clues to help.
2. Who is in this story? Describe the characters.
3. What's happening in this story? What's the big idea?
4. When does this story take place?
5. Where does this story take place?
6. What is the problem in this story? How do you think it will be solved?
7. What does this story make you think about?
8. What is the most important part of this story? Why?
9. What is your favorite part of the story? Why?
10. Would you recommend this story to a friend? Why or why not?

*These questions can be asked through conversation or the child can practice writing skills by answering one or two questions at a time in a journal.

*Research shows that children reading at least 20 minutes a night perform better in school. Pick a time and place that works for your family.

Tackle Reading Tip Page

1. Model reading for your children.
2. Take your children to the library to obtain their own library card.
3. Visit the library or local book store on a regular basis.
4. Read and point out environmental print (labels, signs, boxes, etc.) on outings.
5. Read aloud to your children, no matter their age.
6. Match books to your children's hobbies and interests.
7. Match books to your children's reading levels. Ask your children's teacher for this information.
8. Ask your children questions before, during, and after reading.
9. Start a neighborhood book club for kids and recommend great titles.
10. Keep a reading journal to provide reading responses.

Observation, Evaluation, and Assessment of Readers

Reading is a developmental journey. We can only help our students succeed when we understand their strengths and challenges in reading. This is when data, diagnostic tools, and assessments are valuable. There is nothing worse than a teacher completing an assessment to check it off a list. When we use each tool to determine what to add to our instruction, the one-on-one assessment was worthwhile. Each tool below can be used for a particular purpose in helping the teaching and learning process in literacy be a positive experience for everyone.

- **Concept of Print, Concept of Word, Phonological Awareness, etc.**
- **Reading assessment program (3-4 times a year): Examples may include F &P, DRA, Next Step Guided Reading Assessment, etc.**
- **Running Records (every 3-4 weeks)**
- **Daily observations and anecdotal notes in guided reading**
- **Word Study Inventory: Examples may include *Words Their Way* or *Word Journeys***
- **Words Per Minute Checks**
- **Independent Reading Conferences**
- **Written Reading Responses**
- **Exit Tickets (leveled reading and grade level reading text)**
- **Standardized assessments**

Flexible Guided Reading Groups

Instructional Reading Levels

Teacher's Name_____ Grade _____

Group Members	Reading Level/Skill
1. _____	_____
2. _____	_____
3. _____	_____
4. _____	_____
5. _____	_____
6. _____	_____

Group Members	Reading Level/Skill
1. _____	_____
2. _____	_____
3. _____	_____
4. _____	_____
5. _____	_____
6. _____	_____

Group Members	Reading Level/Skill
1. _____	_____
2. _____	_____
3. _____	_____
4. _____	_____
5. _____	_____
6. _____	_____

Group Members	Reading Level/Skill
1. _____	_____
2. _____	_____
3. _____	_____
4. _____	_____
5. _____	_____
6. _____	_____

Dear Parents/Guardians,
        At this point in the year, your child _____
is reading at the following level:

below benchmark   on benchmark   above benchmark

Attached is a list of book titles that match your child's independent reading level.
Thank you for encouraging nightly reading with a "just right" book.

Dear Parents/Guardians,
        At this point in the year, your child _____
is reading at the following level:

below benchmark   on benchmark   above benchmark

Attached is a list of book titles that match your child's independent reading level.
Thank you for encouraging nightly reading with a "just right" book.

Dear Parents/Guardians,
        At this point in the year, your child _____
is reading at the following level:

below benchmark   on benchmark   above benchmark

Attached is a list of book titles that match your child's independent reading level.
Thank you for encouraging nightly reading with a "just right" book.

I am SMART

(Simply Marvelous At Reading Text)

I am SMART

(Simply Marvelous At Reading Text)

I am SMART

(Simply Marvelous At Reading Text)

I am SMART

(Simply Marvelous At Reading Text)

I am SMART

(Simply Marvelous At Reading Text)

I am SMART

(Simply Marvelous At Reading Text)

'Twas the Night Before Testing
by Kathryn Starke

'Twas the night before testing, when all through the school
Not a teacher was stirring, no one breaking a rule.
The booklets were hung in the office with care,
In hopes that the testing day soon would be there.

The children were nestled all snug in their beds,
While visions of bubbling danced in their heads.
And teachers with clipboards lying flat on their laps
Had just settled their brains for long awaited naps.

When out on the lawn, there arose such a clatter,
The sprang from the chairs to see what was the matter.
Away to the window they flew like a flash,
Tore open the shutters and threw up the sash.

The moon on the roof of the school in the night
Gav the teachers inside some additional light
When what to their wondering eyes should appear
But our principals wearing so much testing gear.

With a really strong driver, I just had to peer
I knew in a moment; our principals were near.
More rapid than mascots, the teachers they came
As they whistled and shouted and called them by name.

Now 1st grade, now 2nd grade, now kindergarten too
On 3rd grade, on 4th, 5th and 6th grade-that's you!
To the top of the roof, to the top of the wall!
Now dash away! Dash away! Dash away all!

They sprang to the office gave the team a big whistle,
And away they all flew like the down of a thistle,
But I heard them explain as they flew out of sight,
Good luck on your testing and to all a good night!

Work Directly with Kathryn Starke
In Your School or District

Kathryn Starke travels throughout the nation to help schools achieve literacy success. She adds her unique techniques and successful strategies to any program. She collaborates with parents, teachers, and administrators in all aspects of reading and writing. Kathryn is available for trainings, presentations, workshops, or consulting sessions in your school, district, organization, or conference. Fees may vary. Contact us for further information to support your educational needs.

Consulting for Schools May Include the Following:

- Plan with reading specialist and/or classroom teachers for weekly and/or quarterly instruction based on district pacing guide
- Conduct data analysis on reading assessments with reading specialist, teachers, and administration to target standard based instruction
- Observe classroom guided reading blocks and provide individual feedback for strengths and challenges in their classroom
- Model reading lessons in the elementary school classroom
- Develop a grade level or school- based language arts curriculum, pacing guide, strategic instructional plan, and reading assessment calendar
- Develop language arts block schedules to include guided reading, shared reading, writing workshop, and word study

Contact: Kathryn Starke, Founder of Creative Minds Publications
Email: info@creativemindspublications.com
Website: www.creativemindspublications.com

Social Media:
Twitter, Instagram, Pinterest, Facebook: @KathrynStarke
Facebook: Facebook.com/creativemindspublications
Shop at https://www.teacherspayteachers.com/Store/Kathryn-Starke

Kathryn Starke is an urban literacy consultant, reading coach, author, keynote speaker, adjunct professor, and founder of Creative Minds Publications. Her educational publishing company creates children's books and educational materials. Starke provides personalized literacy consulting for schools, districts, organizations, and corporations. She graduated from Longwood University with a bachelor's degree in elementary education and a master's degree in Literacy and Culture. Starke's first book, *Amy's Travels*, was the first children's picture book to teach all seven continents. It is used in classrooms in over 26 countries on six continents and was turned into a musical by the Latin Ballet of Virginia. Starke's second book, *Tackle Reading*, is used in an annual educational initiative supported by the NFL and NFL Alumni Association. Starke is a contributing writer for publications including *Edutopia, the 74, Reading Today,* and *Education Post.* Her work has been featured in national media outlets including *Success* magazine, the *New York Post, Thrive Global, Medium,* and *Mashable.* She has provided consulting to help over one hundred elementary schools around country achieve literacy success.

Additional Titles by Kathryn Starke
Amy's Travels
Tackle Reading